Never afraid to tell it like it is, Cas always knows what he's talking ab‹ trademark mix of scholarly experti making us all think twice before we take too much for granted. Genuinely a great read.

Tim Bale, Professor of Politics, Queen Mary University of London, UK

A must-read for anyone interested in this riveting European political moment – populism, freedom of speech, far-right, far-left, religion, Euroscepticism, and euro-crisis. It's all here: well written, provocative, and engaging. Always original and thought-provoking, Cas Mudde combines wonderful political savvy with unrivalled academic expertise.

Catherine Fieschi, Director, Counterpoint, UK

Cas Mudde is the leading public intellectual drawing attention to the challenges to liberal democracy and the European project represented by populist, Eurosceptic parties. Dismissing convenient, simplistic hype over this phenomenon and highlighting the contradictory responses of governments this book defines the issues likely to dominate European politics for years to come.

Geoffrey Harris, European Parliament official (1976–2016) and author of *The Dark Side of Europe*

This collection distils the essential Mudde. His characteristically forthright dissection of key political trends includes a primer on populism that will be widely cited, but he also warns of the dangers of blaming populism for all the problems besetting liberal democracy in Europe today. Mudde's analysis of the damage done by mainstream parties and politicians in the name of combatting extremism should be essential reading for all Europeans worried about the future of democracy and the EU.

Heather Grabbe, Director, Open Society European Policy Institute, Belgium

Cas Mudde is one of the leading specialists of the populist radical right. He is also a man with strong moral and civic values. The pathological normalcy theory he exposes in this collection of his articles is a key to understanding the mounting challenge of the extreme right to liberal democracy. It is also well worth reading his criticism of 'undemocratic liberalism', as the reason for the successes of Left-Wing populism.

Jean-Yves Camus, Directeur de l'Observatoire des radicalités Politiques (ORAP), Paris

On Extremism and Democracy in Europe

On Extremism and Democracy in Europe is a collection of short and accessible essays on the far right, populism, Euroscepticism, and liberal democracy by one of the leading academic and public voices today. It includes both sober, fact-based analysis of the often sensationalized 'rise of the far right' in Europe as well as passionate defence of the fundamental values of liberal democracy. Sometimes counter-intuitive and always thought-provoking, Mudde argues that the true challenge to liberal democracy comes from the political elites at the centre of the political systems rather than from the political challengers at the political margins. Pushing to go beyond the simplistic opposition of extremism and democracy, which is much clearer in theory than in practice, he accentuates the internal dangers of liberal democracy without ignoring the external threats. This book is essential reading for anyone interested in European politics, extremism and/or current affairs more generally.

Cas Mudde is Associate Professor in the School of Public and International Affairs at the University of Georgia, USA and Researcher in the Centre for Research on Extremism (C-REX) at the University of Oslo, Norway.

Routledge Studies in Extremism and Democracy
Series Editors: **Roger Eatwell**, *University of Bath*, and
Matthew Goodwin, *University of Kent.*
Founding Series Editors: Roger Eatwell, *University of Bath*
and **Cas Mudde**, *University of Antwerp-UFSIA.*

This new series encompasses academic studies within the broad fields of
'extremism' and 'democracy'. These topics have traditionally been considered largely in isolation by academics. A key focus of the series, therefore,
is the (inter-)*relation* between extremism and democracy. Works will seek
to answer questions such as to what extent 'extremist' groups pose a major
threat to democratic parties, or how democracy can respond to extremism
without undermining its own democratic credentials.

The books encompass two strands:

Routledge Studies in Extremism and Democracy includes books with an
introductory and broad focus which are aimed at students and teachers. These
books will be available in hardback and paperback. Titles include:

Understanding Terrorism in America
From the Klan to al Qaeda
Christopher Hewitt

Fascism and the Extreme Right
Roger Eatwell

Racist Extremism in Central and Eastern Europe
Edited by Cas Mudde

Political Parties and Terrorist Groups (2nd Edition)
Leonard Weinberg, Ami Pedahzur and Arie Perliger

The New Extremism in 21st Century Britain
Edited by Roger Eatwell and Matthew Goodwin

New British Fascism: Rise of the British National Party
Matthew Goodwin

The End of Terrorism?
Leonard Weinberg

Mapping the Extreme Right in Contemporary Europe:
From Local to Transnational
Edited by Andrea Mammone, Emmanuel Godin and Brian Jenkins

Varieties of Right-Wing Extremism in Europe
Edited by Andrea Mammone, Emmanuel Godin and Brian Jenkins

Right-Wing Radicalism Today
Perspectives from Europe and the US
Edited by Sabine von Mering and Timothy Wyman McCarty

Revolt on the Right
Explaining support for the radical right in Britain
Robert Ford and Matthew Goodwin

Routledge Research in Extremism and Democracy offers a forum for innovative new research intended for a more specialist readership. These books will be in hardback only. Titles include:

On Extremism and Democracy in Europe

Cas Mudde

Routledge
Taylor & Francis Group

LONDON AND NEW YORK

First published 2016
by Routledge

2 Park Square, Milton Park, Abingdon, Oxon OX14 4RN
711 Third Avenue, New York, NY 10017, USA

Routledge is an imprint of the Taylor & Francis Group, an informa business

First issued in paperback 2017

British Library Cataloguing-in-Publication Data
A catalogue record for this book is available from the British Library

Library of Congress Cataloging-in-Publication Data
Names: Mudde, Cas, author.
Title: On extremism and democracy in Europe / Cas Mudde.
Description: Abingdon, Oxon ; New York, NY : Routledge, 2016. |
Series: Routledge studies in extremism and democracy ; 34
Identifiers: LCCN 2015048689| ISBN 9781138651449 (hardback) |
ISBN 9781315622170 (e-book)
Subjects: LCSH: Right-wing extremists—Europe. | Democracy—Europe. |
Political culture—Europe.
Classification: LCC HN380.Z9 R3568 2016 | DDC 303.6094—dc23
LC record available at http://lccn.loc.gov/2015048689

ISBN: 978-1-138-65144-9 (hbk)
ISBN: 978-1-138-71471-7 (pbk)

Typeset in Times New Roman
by Florence Production Ltd, Stoodleigh, Devon, UK

To Maryann

'Our role is simply to be dissidents attempting to make up for the absence of any political opposition.'

Dario Fo, 2002, 'Is this the new fascism?', *Index on Censorship* Vol. 31, No. 2, 2002, p. 82

Contents

PART IV
Liberal democracy 115

Acknowledgements

Chapter 1 was originally published in *Eurozine* (31 August 2010). A longer version was published in *West European Politics*, Vol. 33, No. 6, 2010, pp. 1167–1186.

Chapter 2 is a slightly longer version of an article originally published in *Extremis Project* (20 December 2012). A much longer version was published in *European Journal of Political Research*, Vol. 52, No. 1, 2013, pp. 1–19.

Chapter 3 was originally published in *Open Democracy* (20 August 2013).

Chapter 4 was originally published as 'Russia's Trojan Horse' in *Open Democracy* (8 December 2014).

Chapter 5 was originally published in *Eurozine* (13 March 2015). A longer version will be published as 'Far-right Parties and the 2014 European Elections: Consequences for the Eurosceptic Debate', in Nicholas Startin and Simon Usherwood (eds), *Routledge Handbook on Euroscepticism*. London: Routledge, 2016.

Chapter 6 was originally published as 'Why the New Far-Right Political Group in the European Parliament is a Political Failure' in *Open Democracy* (16 June 2015).

Chapter 7 is a longer version of pieces that were published in *Eutopia* (14 September 2015) and in the *Washington Post* (10 August 2015).

Chapter 8 was originally published in the *Washington Post* (30 December 2014).

Chapter 9 was originally published in *The Guardian* (17 February 2015).

Chapter 10 was originally published in *Open Democracy* (29 April 2015).

Chapter 11 is a slightly longer version of an article originally published in *Open Democracy* (12 May 2015).

Chapter 12 was originally published in *Open Democracy* (24 May 2011).

Chapter 13 was originally published in *Open Democracy* (18 March 2013).

Chapter 14 was originally published in *Balkans in Europe Policy Blog* (20 May 2014).

Chapter 15 was originally published as 'The European Parliament Elections Show the Increasingly Fragmented Nature of European Party Systems' in *LSE EUROPP* (12 June 2014).

Chapter 16 was originally published in *Open Democracy* (11 June 2015).

Chapter 17 was originally published in *Open Democracy* (23 July 2015).

Chapter 18 was originally published in *Open Democracy* (13 July 2015).

Chapter 19 was originally published in *Huffington Post* (16 March 2015).

Chapter 20 was originally published in the *Washington Post* (28 October 2014).

Chapter 21 was originally published in *Eurozine* (24 August 2011).

Chapter 22 was originally published in *Today's Zaman* (17 August 2011).

Chapter 23 was originally published in *Open Democracy* (28 August 2012).

Chapter 24 was originally published as 'Liberal Democracy: The Do's and Don'ts of Banning Political Extremism' in *Open Democracy* (11 August 2014).

Chapter 25 was originally published in *Open Democracy* (7 January 2015).

Chapter 26 was originally published in *Open Democracy* (11 February 2015).

Chapter 27 was originally published in *Open Democracy* (26 October 2015).

A shorter version of the epilogue was originally published in *Open Democracy* (1 December 2015).

Preface

I don't know exactly when I wrote my first article for a newspaper, but I do know it was when I was getting my PhD in political science at Leiden University. I am sure it was on the radical right in the Netherlands, a topic that was constantly in the Dutch media at that time, but was hardly studied – to be fair, there was not too much to study at that time. The idea that (social) scientists would contribute to the public debate through columns, interviews and op-eds was shared among virtually all of my professors, which included nationally recognized columnists and opinion makers like Koen Koch (*Trouw* and *Volkskrant*), Margo Trappenburg (*NRC Handelsblad*), and Bart Tromp (*Parool*).

So far I have remained a columnist without a column, much less consequential than my Leiden professors, but not less passionate. I guess I write op-eds for a variety of reasons. Having worked primarily at public universities, albeit in many different countries, I strongly believe that academics should make their work available and useful to the broader public, which, in the end, pays their salaries. This can be done in many different forms, but for a political scientist working on contemporary issues, articles and interviews in the media are a very direct and effective form. Obviously, it is not all about the public good. I am a highly opinionated person, even for a Dutchman, and writing op-eds is also a therapeutic activity for me. Even if no one reads my articles, or is swayed by them, they still serve an important purpose to me. Finally, few academics are without a sizeable ego, and I am certainly no exception. Hence, I also write op-eds in the hope to one day become that grand, if increasingly outdated, ideal of the true European academic: the public intellectual.

This book is a collection of my writings on the four key topics of my academic work: the far right, populism, European politics, and liberal democracy. Obviously, the four overlap, and all tie into the key question underlying my academic work, as well as my personal political concerns: *how can a liberal democracy defend itself against political challenge(r)s without undermining its own core values?* Although I have always been concerned about state infringements on liberal protections, notably free speech, the aftermath of 9/11 has made the issue more central to me. What the response to 9/11 showed on a global scale, and the killing of Theo van Gogh did on a national scale, is that when the enemy is constructed as threatening enough, people can be very easily swayed to give up some of their fundamental rights. The key is to sell it as if only 'their,' i.e. the 'extremists' or 'terrorists', rights are affected, not 'ours,' i.e. the moderate law-abiding citizen. And so, the left supports infringements upon the (far) right's rights, and the right supports infringements upon the (far) left's rights, not understanding that each time the rights of *all*, including themselves, are curtailed.

This is also why I became interested in the far right. I saw that liberal democrats were calling for the restriction of the rights of far right activists and parties, including the right to free speech and to organize, arguing that 'democracy' was in danger. But I did not see the far right danger. It would take me many more years to fully comprehend the differences between democracy and liberal democracy, and between radical and extreme challengers. And as the main enemy changed from the 'extreme right' to 'extreme Muslims,' the pressure on the core values of liberal democracy became more intense and more threatening.

Europeans too often prefer to look only to the US as the root of all their, and the world's, political problems. But while the PATRIOT ACT and 'War on Terror' are indeed very striking examples of state overreach, most European democracies responded much the same, but often with fewer and weaker constitutional protections. Because where the US has at least some established and reasonably effective non-governmental organizations to challenge the state, like the American Civil Liberties Union (ACLU), most Europeans are dependent upon (semi-)state institutions like the Ombudsmen.

In essence, this book is about democracy, more specifically liberal democracy in Europe. Whether expressed explicitly or assumed implicitly, the challenge to liberal democracy is the main reason for the long-standing academic and public obsession with the far right and with populism. But my focus is not just on the ways in which far right and populist groups, mostly political parties, challenge European democracies, but on how mainstream parties, (allegedly) responding to far right and populist challenges, threaten core values of liberal democracy. This is also my main interest in the debate on European integration, as far as one can speak of a debate. While I have strong (increasingly negative) opinions about the process of European integration in general, and the institution of the European Union (EU) in particular, my main interest is in how they are affecting liberal democracy in Europe.

Although I feel that my ideals have remained fairly stable since I wrote my first op-eds in graduate school, the political context in Europe has changed significantly since then. Where I was considered a sceptic about immigration and multi-ethnic societies in the politically correct Netherlands of the late 1980s, I would probably be labelled a naive utopian 'multikulti' in my home country today. Obviously, the change in the public mood and political debate is not unrelated to actual events, such as the rise of Jihadist terrorism or the Great Recession – even if the political and public discourse around the events were more influential than the actual facts. As 2001 was a year that changed the United States, because of the terrorist attacks of 9/11, I feel that 2015 has been a year that has changed Europe forever.

In many ways 2015 is Europe's *annus horribilis* (horrible year). Many Europeans lost their last shred of belief in, or hope for, an integrated and multicultural Europe that year. The Greek economic crisis led to an out-pouring of new anti-EU sentiment among the moderate left, while the refugees crisis has had a similar effect among the moderate right. The frustration and disillusionment of ever-growing groups of the European people is mostly caused by the actions and inactions of the European political elites, who, when their lofty ideals are confronted with concrete problems, quickly abandon their moral high ground and hide behind the alleged preferences of the populations – the same preferences and populations that until that time had been decried as 'racist' by those very same political elites.

Most disturbingly, while far too much was decried as 'racist' in the 1980s, far too much is embraced as 'realistic' today. In 1982 the Dutch Christian Democratic Appeal (CDA) denounced the 'neo-fascist' Center Party (CP) of Hans Janmaat – whose most controversial statement was 'The Netherlands is full. Stop immigration.' In 2010 the same CDA joined the minority government of conservative Prime Minister Mark Rutte, supported by the Party for Freedom (PVV) of Geert Wilders – who wants to stop all immigration from Muslim countries. And in October 2015 representatives of the CDA applauded at the Madrid Congress of the European People's Party (EPP) as Hungarian Prime Minister Viktor Orbán likened the Syrian refugees to an invading army and accuses the left-wing parties of welcoming immigrants as a plot to increase their electorate – a popular far right conspiracy theory that Janmaat used against both the social democratic Labor Party (PvdA) and the CDA in the 1980s!

In this transformed political context I have found myself increasingly on the side of those I have criticized for decades: the so-called alarmists. While I continue to believe that the success and threat of traditional far right parties like the National Front (FN) of Marine Le Pen is exaggerated in the media, and in much of the academic writing, there is no doubt that far right parties have become a (and perhaps *the*) main political actor in *some* European countries – notably Austria, Denmark, France, Switzerland. Of more importance, however, is the much less noted growing prominence of far right politics, mainly pushed through by actors other than the usual suspects. As I argue in several articles in this book, it is the growing elite support for the far right politics of 'mainstream' politicians like Orbán that is much more threatening for European liberal democracy than the growing mass support for far right politicians like Le Pen.

All chapters in this book were originally published in online media. In most cases I made only minor stylistic changes to the original version. In some cases I included a more elaborate version, often the first version, which was cut due to space constraints. I decided not to update the articles, with some notable exceptions in endnotes, as they are to be understood in the political context in which they were written. I want to thank all the editors that I have been working with at the various outlets, most notably Ben Tendler at *Eurozine*, Katherine Butler and Philip Oltermann at *The Guardian*, Nikos Agouros and Nick Miriello at the *Huffington Post*, Stuart Brown at LSE's *EUROPP* blog, Rosemary Bechler, David Krivanek, and Alex Sakalis at *Open Democracy*, and EJ Graff, John Sides, and Erik Voeten at the Monkey Cage (*Washington Post*). Special thanks to Antonis Galanopoulos for his highly critical but respectful interview.

This book also gives me the chance to finally express my immense gratitude to Craig Fowlie, editor extraordinaire at Routledge, and the inspiration of this book. Craig contacted Roger Eatwell and I more than fifteen years ago with the idea to start a book series at Routledge. Today the Routledge Studies in Extremism and Democracy is the preeminent book series on the topic, capably edited by Roger and, my successor, Matthew Goodwin. Craig has not only been a loyal patron of the book series and of my own work at Routledge, he has also been one of my favorite people in the political science circuit, with whom I always try to have lunch or a drink at conferences, to discuss the finer things of life, i.e. football and punk music.

Finally, I want to thank my colleague and wife, Maryann Gallagher, whose patience and tolerance I have been testing for almost ten years now – a price she pays for having taken me away from my beloved Antwerp. As my life partner she bears the brunt of my obsessive need to share my opinions with the world. How often has she had to hear my rants on yet another article that came to me in the shower? Not only does she tolerate my op-eds, she often edits them, pushing me to clarify and elaborate as I nervously and tensely look over her shoulder. This book is for you, my love!

Part I
The far right

1 The populist radical right

A pathological normalcy

> Today the politics of the radical right is the politics of frustration – the sour impotence of those who find themselves unable to understand, let alone command, the complex mass society that is the polity today.[1]

The quote above could have been from any recent book on the contemporary radical right, but actually dates from 1962, and summarizes the famed American sociologist Daniel Bell's assessment of the US radical right in the 1950s. It is typical of a variety of dominant positions in the academic debate on the populist radical right, which might be referred to as the 'normal pathology thesis.' This thesis holds that the radical right constitutes a pathology in post-war western society and that its success is to be explained by crisis. Authors working within this paradigm often consider the radical right in psychological terms and regularly use medical and psychological concepts to define and explain it.

However, the normal pathology thesis cannot withstand empirical testing: far from being an aberration, the attitudes and ideological features of the populist radical right are fairly widespread in contemporary European societies. Instead of being understood as a normal pathology, the contemporary populist radical right needs to be seen as a pathological normalcy. This change of perspective has important consequences for how we should study and understand the contemporary populist radical right.

The normal pathology thesis explained

According to most scholarship on the populist radical right, radicalism in general and extremism in particular are based upon values that are fundamentally opposed to those of (western) democracy. In his political–historical study of political extremism, the German political scientist Uwe Backes defines extremism as antithetical to democracy.[2] However, it would be more accurate to describe radicalism as democratic, but anti-liberal-democratic.[3] Consequently, both extremism and radicalism challenge the fundamental values of contemporary western societies.

Much scholarship on the 'far' (i.e. extreme and radical) right goes beyond the ideological opposition between radicalism and democracy and considers the far right (in its various permutations) in psychological terms, mostly as a pathology of modern society. The most influential studies in this tradition are the psychoanalytical analyses of fascism, such as Wilhelm Reich's *The Mass Psychology of Fascism* (1933) and Theodor W. Adorno and his collaborators' *The Authoritarian Personality* (1950). Given that research on the post-war radical right was heavily influenced by studies of historical fascism, it comes as no surprise that the pathology approach also dominates that field.

This is particularly the case with early scholarship on the post-war American radical right. Bell's classic article 'The Dispossessed' provides an analysis of the 'psychological stock-in-trade' of the radical right, rather than its ideology, and is filled with references to pathologies such as paranoia and conspiracy thinking.[4] Similarly, the progressive US American historian Richard Hofstadter argued that the radical right 'stands psychologically outside the frame of normal democratic politics.'[5]

Many studies of the contemporary radical right in Europe have followed suit. References to paranoia and other psychological disorders abound in politically inspired studies that unfortunately still occupy a prominent position in the field (particularly in Germany and France). Even in serious research populist radical right parties and their supporters are often perceived in terms of a normal pathology.[6]

The German social scientists Erwin Scheuch and Hans Klingemann developed a 'theory of rightwing radicalism in western industrial societies' in the late 1960s, which is still one of the most ambitious and comprehensive attempts at explaining the political success of radical right parties in postwar Europe – notably Germany – to date.[7] In short, they hold that populist radical right values are alien to western democratic values, but that a small potential exists for them in all western societies; hence, they are a 'normal pathology.' Within this paradigm, support for populist radical right parties is based on 'structurally determined pathologies.'

Normal pathology and academic research

The normal pathology paradigm has had profound effects on the academic study of the populist radical right. In its most extreme form, scholars study the phenomenon in isolation from mainstream democratic politics, i.e. without using mainstream concepts and theories. According to this approach, the populist radical right is a pathology and can only be explained outside of the normal. In most cases, this decision is as much political as it is methodological: to use mainstream concepts and theories, the researchers argue, is to legitimize the populist radical right.

This extreme interpretation was particularly prevalent in the study of the populist radical right in France, Germany and the Netherlands in the 1980s and 1990s. Many authors would focus almost exclusively on the populist radical right's connection to pre-war fascism and Nazism. The assumption was that the post-war populist radical right had to be understood as a remnant of the past, not a consequence of contemporary developments.

The more moderate form has always dominated studies of the electoral success of the populist radical right, and has become popular through the works of scholars who integrated insights from the study of political parties (most notably the Greens). This school of studies employs mainstream concepts and theories, but still perceives the populist radical right as an anomaly of contemporary western democracies.

The key puzzle in the normal pathology paradigm is the question as to why popular demand for populist radical right politics exists. Two general answers are offered – protest and support – though both are based upon a similar assumption: that under 'normal' circumstances the demand for populist radical right politics comes from only a tiny part of the population. Hence, the search was on for those abnormal circumstances in which populist radical right attitudes spread. Most scholars find the answer in modern interpretations of the classic modernization thesis.

Almost all major versions of the normal pathology thesis refer to some form of crisis linked to modernization and its consequences: globalization, the post-Fordist economy, postindustrial society. The idea is always the same: society is transforming fundamentally and rapidly, leading to a division between (self-perceived) winners and losers, and the latter will vote for the populist radical right out of protest (anger and frustration) or support (intellectual rigidity). Under conditions of massive societal change, the 'losers of modernization' vote for populist radical right parties.

In this approach, populist radical right parties – and political actors in general – hardly play a role. The only internal (f)actor that is sometimes included is charismatic leadership. This derives from the famous German sociologist Max Weber's theory of charismatic leadership, although few authors refer explicitly to Weber, and is in full accordance with the pathology thesis. As in 'normal' politics, voting should be rational, based on ideology, or at least identity (cleavage), and not on an irrational bond with an individual.

In short, studies applying the normal pathology thesis tend to approach the populist radical right from the perspective of either fascism (extreme) or crisis (moderate). The prime focus is on explaining demand, which under 'normal' conditions is supposed to be low. The supply-side of politics is almost completely ignored, as is the role of the populist radical right itself. When internal supply does enter the equation, it is in the form of charismatic leadership, again perceived as a pathological remnant of a dark past.

The normal pathology thesis assessed

But is the ideological core of the populist radical right – defined as a combination of nativism, authoritarianism and populism – indeed at odds with the basic values of western societies? And are populist radical right values really shared by only a tiny minority of the European population?

The ideological

The key feature of the populist radical right ideology is nativism: an ideology which holds that states should be inhabited exclusively by members of the native group ('the nation') and that non-native elements (persons and ideas) are fundamentally threatening to the nation-state's homogeneity. Nativist thinking has a long history in western societies, notably in the US, with movements like the Know Nothings dating back to the early nineteenth century.

Historically and ideologically, nativism is closely linked to the idea of the nation-state, a nationalist construction that has become a cornerstone of European and global politics. The idea of the nation-state holds that each nation should have its own state and, although this is often left implicit, each state should have its own, single nation. Various European constitutions stipulate that their state is linked to one specific nation; for example, the Slovak preamble starts with 'We, the Slovak nation,' while article 4.1 of the Romanian constitution states that 'the foundation of the state is based on the unity of the Romanian people.' The idea of national self-determination is even enshrined in Chapter 1, article 1 of the United Nations Charter, which explicitly calls for respect for the 'self-determination of peoples.'

This is not to claim that all references to national self-determination are necessarily expressions of nativism. For example, article 1 of the Constitution of Ireland states:

> The Irish nation hereby affirms its inalienable, indefeasible, and sovereign right to choose its own form of Government, to determine its relations with other nations, and to develop its life, political, economic and cultural, in accordance with its own genius and traditions.

However, further articles express a fairly open attitude to non-natives, including 'the firm will of the Irish Nation, in harmony and friendship, to unite all the people who share the territory of the island of Ireland, in all the diversity of their identities and traditions' (article 3).

But even where European states are not nativist, they will use 'banal nationalism,' a term used by the British sociologist Michael Billig to refer to everyday 'ideological habits which enable the established nations of the West to be reproduced.'[8] Citizens in western countries are daily reminded of their 'national identity' through a plethora of more and less subtle hints, ranging from the celebration of Independence Day, through the name of media outlets (e.g. *Irish* Times, *British* Broadcasting Corporation, *Hrvatska* Radio Televizija), to history education in schools. Although banal reminders, they are based on the constituting idea of the nation-state.

Authoritarianism, the belief in a strictly ordered society in which infringements of authority are to be punished severely, is not exclusive to the core of populist radical right ideology. Most notably, 'love and respect for authority,' a euphemistic description of authoritarianism, is considered to be a core staple of conservatism. Moreover, authoritarianism is a key aspect of both secular and religious thinking, ranging from (proto-)liberals like Thomas Hobbes to socialists like Vladimir Ilyich Lenin, and from Roman Catholicism to Orthodox Christianity.

The third and final feature is populism, here defined as a thin-centred ideology that considers society to be ultimately separated into two homogeneous and antagonistic groups, 'the pure people' versus 'the corrupt elite.' It argues that politics should be an expression of the *volonté générale*, i.e. the general will of the people. While the populist ideology has much deeper roots in the US than in (Western) Europe, key elements are clearly linked to fundamental values of western societies in general.

Democracy has a redemptive and a pragmatic side: the former emphasizes the idea (1) of *vox populi vox dei* – or 'government of the people, by the people, for the people' – the latter the importance of institutions. As the British political theorist Margaret Canovan has argued, 'inherent in modern democracy, in tension with its pragmatic face, is faith in secular redemption: the promise of a better world through action by the sovereign people.'[9] Populism builds upon this 'democratic promise.' Interpreting 'the people' as a homogenous moral entity, populists argue that *the* common sense of *the* people should always take precedence and cannot be curtailed by 'undemocratic' institutional constraints such as constitutional protection of minorities.

Populism's anti-establishment sentiments are closely connected to broadly shared beliefs in western societies. These range from Lord Acton's famous adagio 'power corrupts' to the negative image of humanity so essential to Christianity (e.g. in the Original Sin). Indeed, the fact that Evangelical Christianity plays a much greater role in US culture and politics than in

Europe might be part of the explanation of the broader and deeper anti-establishment sentiments in that country. Moreover, whereas the process of democratization and state formation in much of Western Europe was more elite-driven, based upon a strong central authority and an elitist distrust of the people, in the US the same processes were driven, at least in the dominant national narrative, by 'We, the People of the United States,' and by a distrust in central government shared by both the masses and the elites, including the Founding Fathers.

The attitudinal

Although nativism is not the same as racism, cross-national surveys such as the Eurobarometer provide ample evidence of extreme nativist attitudes in Europe.[10] For example, Eurobarometer 47.1 (1997) found that 'only one in three of those interviewed said they felt they were 'not at all racist.' One in three declared themselves 'a little racist' and one third openly expressed 'quite or very racist feelings.'

More concretely, 65 per cent of the EU-15 people agree with the statement, 'Our country has reached its limits; if there were to be more people belonging to these minority groups we would have problems.'[11] Almost two-thirds believe that all illegal immigrants should be sent back, while 80 per cent believe illegal immigrants 'convicted of serious offences' should be repatriated. Going beyond what even (most) populist radical right parties demand, some 20 per cent support 'wholesale repatriation,' agreeing with the statement that 'all immigrants, whether legal or illegal, from outside the EU and their children, even those born here, should be sent back to their country of origin.'

In terms of authoritarianism, surveys show an even stronger overlap between mass attitudes and populist radical right positions. According to Eurobarometer 66 (2006), 78 per cent of EU-15 citizens believe that young people would commit less crime if they were better disciplined at home or at school, ranging from 65 per cent in Austria to 90 per cent in France. Similarly, 62 per cent of EU-15 citizens believe that young people would commit less crime if prison sentences were tougher, ranging from 37 per cent in Sweden to 75 per cent in Ireland. Although 55 per cent of EU citizens think their local police 'are doing a good job,' 74 per cent believe that 'better policing' would reduce crime in their area. Finally, a staggering 85 per cent of the EU-25 population agrees with the statement: 'Nowadays there is too much tolerance. Criminals should be punished more severely.' This ranges from 70 per cent in Denmark to 97 per cent to Cyprus.

The ideological nature of populism can only be studied through its anti-elitist or anti-establishment aspect. As the booming literature on

Politikverdrossenheit (political apathy) has argued, and partly proven, growing groups of EU citizens hold negative attitudes towards the main institutions of their national democratic system, though not towards the democratic system as such. In fact, according to Eurobarometer 52 (2000), 40 per cent of EU-15 citizens were 'not very satisfied' or 'not at all satisfied' with their national democracy, ranging from 70 per cent in Italy to 22 per cent in the Netherlands. Eurobarometer 59 (2003) reported that 46 per cent of EU-15 respondents claimed that they 'tend not to trust' their national parliament, 53 per cent claiming the same for the national government, and a staggering 75 per cent for political parties, the main institutions of European democracies.

Regarding corruption, a prominent staple of populist radical right propaganda, Eurobarometer 245 (2006) found that 72 per cent of EU-25 citizens believe that corruption is a major problem in their country. 59 per cent believe that giving or receiving bribes is not successfully prosecuted. Of the political and societal sectors that are believed to be corrupt, 'politicians at national level' top the list, according to 60 per cent of the EU-25 respondents, ranging from 29 per cent in Denmark to 69 per cent in Slovenia. Politicians at the regional level (47 per cent) and at the local level (45 per cent) are ranked fourth and fifth.

From normal pathology to pathological normalcy

The preceding analysis has shown that the normal pathology thesis does not hold up to empirical scrutiny. Populist radical right ideas are not alien to the mainstream ideologies of western democracy and populist radical right attitudes are not just shared by a tiny minority of the European population. In fact, the populist radical right is better perceived as a *pathological normalcy*, to stay within the terminology of Scheuch and Klingemann. It is well connected to mainstream ideas and much in tune with broadly shared attitudes and policy positions.

The pathological normalcy thesis does not entail that the populist radical right is *part* of the mainstream of contemporary democratic societies. Rather, it holds that, ideologically and attitudinally, the populist radical right constitutes a radicalization of mainstream views. The argument is that *key aspects* of the populist radical right ideology are shared by the mainstream, both at the elite and mass levels, albeit often in a more moderate form. Not surprisingly, this has a profound influence on how we should understand the relationship between the populist radical right and western democracy. The key difference between the populist radical right and western democracy is not to be defined *in kind*, i.e. by antithesis, but *in degree*, i.e. by moderate versus radical versions of roughly the same views.[12]

Pathological normalcy and academic research

The paradigmatic shift from normal pathology to pathological normalcy has profound consequences for the academic study of the populist radical right. First and foremost, it means that the populist radical right should be studied on the basis of concepts and theories of mainstream political science. Second, the primary focus of the research should not be on explaining demand, since this is generated naturally by the complex multiethnic western democracies, but on explaining supply.

For the populist radical right, the political struggle is not so much about attitudes as about issues. Although the populist radical right trinity of issues – corruption-immigration-security – are shared to a great extent by a significant part of the population, 'their' issues have not on the whole dominated the political debate in western democracies. Populist radical right parties do not focus primarily on socio-economic issues, like most traditional parties, but on socio-cultural issues, much like that other new party family, the Greens.

Within the pathological normalcy paradigm, understanding the success and failure of the populist radical right depends on understanding the struggle over issue *saliency* and *positions*. To borrow the terminology of the Dutch political scientist Paul Lucardie, populist radical right parties are 'purifiers' that refer to an ideology that has been 'betrayed or diluted' by established parties, rather than 'prophets' that articulate 'a new ideology.'[13] They do not have to sway voters to a new position, but shift them to a new issue: away from socio-economic issues, like (un)employment, and towards socio-cultural issues like immigration. The main struggle of populist radical right parties is to increase the saliency of 'their' issues, i.e. corruption, immigration, and security.

The increasing electoral success for populist radical right parties since the mid-1980s is to a large extent explained by the broader shift away from classic materialist politics towards some form of so-called post-materialist politics, or at least a combination of the two. Within this process, the populist radical right played only a marginal role. Rather, it was to a large extent an unintended reaction to the success of the New Left in the late 1960s and 1970s, which led to a neoconservative backlash in the late 1970s and 1980s. This development not only created electoral space for the populist radical right, it opened up a new and 'level' playing field for competition over socio-cultural issues such as corruption, immigration and security.

The fact that some populist radical right parties have been able to use these opportunities while others have not can be explained by the concept of 'issue ownership' or, more accurately, *issue position ownership*.[14] While the new playing field was level in all countries, the struggle for issue position ownership varied. In some countries, new or reformed (right-wing) parties could capture issue position ownership on corruption, immigration, and security before a populist radical right party was able to establish itself. In most cases, however, a lack of organization and personnel within the populist radical right parties prevented them from achieving issue position ownership. They were haunted by internal strife and public scandal, making them an unattractive political actor despite their advantageous issue position.

Where the populist radical right was able to establish issue position ownership, the key explanation for their success was internal. While it was mostly the established parties, forced by the public and the media, that created the conditions for the electoral breakthrough of populist radical right parties, they themselves ensured their electoral persistence through a combination of leadership, organization, and propaganda. That said, much more empirical study is needed to get a clearer view on what exactly distinguishes successful and unsuccessful party organization, leadership and propaganda.

Conclusion

The study of the populist radical right has been dominated by the normal pathology thesis, i.e. the belief that the populist radical right is a pathology of contemporary western democracies that has only limited support under normal circumstances. Within this paradigm, mass demand for populist radical right parties is the main conundrum and can only be explained by some form of modernization theory-related crisis.

However the normal pathology thesis does not hold up under empirical scrutiny. The key features of the populist radical right ideology – nativism, authoritarianism, and populism – are not unrelated to mainstream ideologies and mass attitudes. In fact, they are best seen as a radicalization of mainstream values. Hence, the populist radical right should be considered a pathological normalcy, not a normal pathology.

This paradigmatic shift has profound consequences for the study and understanding of the populist radical right. Widespread demand is a given, rather than the puzzle, in contemporary western democracies. Provocatively stated, the real question is not why populist radical right parties have been so successful since the 1980s, but why so *few* parties have profited from the fertile breeding ground available to them. The answer is to be found in the supply-side of issue politics, most notably in the struggles over the saliency of issues (particularly for the phase of electoral breakthrough) and over issue position ownership (especially for the phase of electoral persistence). This can only be truly understood if the populist radical right itself is brought back into the analysis and explanation.

Notes

1 Daniel Bell, 'The Dispossessed', in Daniel Bell (ed.), *The Radical Right*. Garden City, NY: Anchor, 1964, p. 42.
2 See Uwe Backes, *Politischer Extremismus in demokratischen Verfassungs-staaten. Elemente einer Rahmentheorie*. Opladen, Germany: Westdeutscher, 1989; *Political Extremes: A Conceptual History from Antiquity to the Present.* London: Routledge, 2011.
3 If not indicated differently, most of the definitions used in this book are taken from: Cas Mudde, *Populist Radical Right Parties in Europe*. Cambridge: Cambridge University Press, 2007, Chapter 1.
4 Bell, 'The Dispossessed'.
5 Richard Hofstadter, 'Pseudo-Conservatism Revisited: A Postscript', in Daniel Bell (ed.), *The Radical Right*. Garden City, NY: Anchor, 1964, p. 102.
6 For contemporary authors working in this tradition, see Hans-Georg Betz, *Radical Right-Wing Populism in Western Europe*. Basingstoke, UK: Macmillan, 1994; Frank Decker, *Der neue Rechtspopulismus.* Opladen, Germany: Leske + Budrich, 2004; Michael Minkenberg, *Die neue radikale Rechte im Vergleich. USA, Frankreich, Deutschland.* Opladen: Westdeutscher, 1998.
7 Erwin K. Scheuch and Hans D. Klingemann, 'Theorie des Rechtsradikalismus in westlichen Industriegesellschaften', *Hamburger Jahrbuch für Wirtschafts- und Gesellschaftspolitik*, Vol. 12, 1967, pp. 11–19. It should be noted that this description of the normal pathology thesis is not to be seen as a summary of their entire theory, but rather of one aspect of it – an aspect that has been much more influential than the rest of the theoretical framework.
8 Michael Billig, *Banal Nationalism*. London: Sage, 1995, p. 6.
9 Margaret Canovan, 'Trust the People! Populism and the Two Faces of Democracy', *Political Studies*, Vol. 47, No. 1, 1999, p. 11.
10 The Eurobarometer is a series of cross-national surveys of EU member states that has been conducted by the European Commission since 1973. All Euro-barometer studies can be found online at http://ec.europa.eu/public_opinion/index_en.htm.
11 EU-12 refers to the EU between 1980 and 1995, when it included the following twelve member states: Belgium, Denmark, France, Germany, Greece, Ireland, Italy, Luxembourg, Netherlands, Portugal, Spain and the United Kingdom. In 1995, Austria, Finland and Sweden joined, transforming it into the EU-15. In 2004, ten new, mainly East European countries joined (Cyprus, Czech Republic, Estonia, Hungary, Latvia, Lithuania, Malta, Poland, Slovakia and Slovenia), making it the EU-25. With the addition of Bulgaria and Romania, in 2007, the European Union became the EU-27. The last country to join was Croatia, in 2013, which made it the EU-28.
12 How broadly shared the populist radical right ideology is, cannot yet be established on the basis of the available data. This would require a complex measurement model, encompassing a collection of multiple indictors for all three (multifaceted) ideological features, rather than simplistic indicators like left-right self-placement or support for racist movements.
13 Paul Lucardie, 'Prophets, Purifiers and Prolocutors: Towards a Theory on the Emergence of New Parties', *Party Politics*, Vol. 6, No. 2, 2000, p. 175.
14 In short, party A *owns* position X (on issue Y) when a large part of the electorate that (1) cares about issue Y and (2) holds position X, trusts party A to be the most competent party to shift policies (directly or indirectly) towards issue position X.

2 Three decades of populist radical right parties in Western Europe
So what?

The populist radical right constitutes the most successful new party family in postwar Western Europe. Many accounts in both academia and the media warn of the growing influence of populist radical right parties, the so-called *verrechtsing* (right turn) of European politics, but few provide empirical evidence of it. In a recent publication[1] I have provided a first comprehensive analysis of the alleged effects of populist radical right parties on the people, parties, policies and polities of Western Europe.

The conclusions are sobering. The effects are largely limited to the broader immigration issue, and even here populist radical right parties should be seen as *catalysts* rather than initiators, who are neither a necessary nor a sufficient condition for the introduction of stricter immigration policies. I would here like to focus on two aspects: explain the limited impact of populist radical right parties and shortly assess their future.

A turn to the right . . . but which right?

Michael Minkenberg's apt summary of the essential impact of populist radical right parties on European democracies, based on a very limited set of cases and made over ten years ago, still holds good: 'The "government of the people, by the people, for the people" is not at stake, but the concept of the "people" is.'[2] As far as there has been influence, it has been on redefining the people; or, more accurately, re-redefining the people in the manner that they had always been implicitly defined in the pre-multicultural society, namely as ethnically homogeneous. This influence has been mostly indirect, and in line with the democratic process, in the sense that populist radical right parties politicized existing anti-immigrant sentiments in the population, which encouraged mainstream parties – if encouragement was needed – to adopt their issues and issue position, albeit in a more moderate form, and change policies accordingly.

However, although some populist radical right parties may be seen as *catalysts* in this process, they are neither a necessary nor a sufficient condition. Their success was enabled by the pre-existence of a fertile breeding ground of popular resentment around immigration, crime, and party politics across Western Europe (see Chapter 1). In fact, mainstream right-wing parties are more responsible for the recent anti-immigration turn than populist radical right parties. While all have moved to a more strict immigration and integration position, some have chosen to use this particular issue to gain governmental power by co-opting either the populist radical right parties or their voters. In most of these cases, the mainstream right adopted not just a more radical immigration position, but also implemented more strict immigration policies than in other countries.

European integration, like immigration, was for long a taboo issue in European politics, often consciously excluded from the political agenda by the political elites. However, unlike immigration, European integration could for decades rely on a permissive consensus at the mass level. Since the early 1990s, however, popular support for European integration has decreased, sharply in some countries, even if outright rejection of the idea has increased more modestly. It is unlikely that populist radical right parties played an important role in the rise of Euroscepticism at the elite and mass level. First, much of the critique is related to new developments: as the EU has become more defined, more people and parties see particular things wrong with it. Second, most of the more outspoken Eurosceptic parties today developed their position independent of, and often well before, the relevance of the populist radical right. And, third, strong opposition to aspects of European integration comes at least as much from other political actors, including radical left parties and trade unions – as was the case in the Dutch and French referendums on the so-called 'European Constitution' in 2005.

Populist radical right parties have been even less relevant for the authoritarian turn in Western Europe. The turn started in most countries in the 1980s, as a consequence of neoconservative influence within the mainstream right (and sometimes left), well before the populist radical right started to gain significant electoral support. And while populist radical right parties have been strong supporters of strict anti-terrorism legislation, the post-9/11 securitization of politics was broadly supported within the political mainstream and needed neither the initiative nor the support of them.

Finally, related to their anti-establishment discourse, many populist radical right parties call for the introduction of plebiscitarian measures to 'democratize' the political systems and break the power of 'the corrupt political establishment.' They do not seem to have been very successful, or forceful, on this issue, however. While the number of national referenda in Western Europe has increased, most were related to European integration and were either constitutionally required or the consequence of pressure from other political actors.

In short, while the *verrechtsing* thesis seems correct in terms of a move to more right-wing positions on the socio-cultural dimension at the mass and elite level, it is wrong on the main cause of this process. Rather than the populist radical right, it has been the mainstream right-wing that has pushed West European politics to the right, in part in response to media and popular responses to relatively recent developments (such as multi-ethnic societies, the Maastricht Treaty and 9/11). In many cases, the mainstream left has proven either incompetent to halt the turn or remarkably collaborative in supporting it.

Explaining the limited impact of populist radical right parties

One of the main reasons for the limited impact of populist radical right parties is that they are mostly 'purifiers' rather than 'prophets,' i.e. they push for policy changes on existing issues, not for new ones, like the Greens did with the environment (see also Chapter 1). On many issues the mainstream parties had already done much of the groundwork before populist radical right parties were strong enough to challenge them. A good example is the alleged new issue of immigration control. Most West European countries had by and large banned economic immigration in 1973–4, as a response to the oil crisis, well before immigration control became politicized and populist radical right parties gained their first significant electoral successes (in the late 1980s). These policies had largely been considered technical measures and were silently approved by political actors across the political spectrum.

The most obvious reason for the limited impact, however, is the relatively modest electoral support that these parties generate in parliamentary elections. With an average support of less than ten per cent of the electorate, few populist radical right parties are major players in their national political system. Moreover, even fewer make it into government, majority or minority, and most are shunned by the other parties in parliament. Hence, direct policy influence is already quite rare. And even when populist radical right parties make it into power, they are dogs that bark loud, but hardly ever bite.

There are at least five reasons for the governmental impotence of populist radical right parties. First, these parties focus on only *a few issues*, significantly reducing the scope of their impact, even if successful. Second, political parties are just *one of many actors* in creating policies; bureaucracies and non-governmental actors severely limit the room to maneuver for parties (particularly for populist radical right parties, which have few supporters in the major policy networks). Third, populist radical right parties are always *junior parties* in coalition, much less experienced than both their coalition partners and the other actors within the policy networks. Fourth, coalition governments are the outcomes of processes of *policy convergence* between mainstream and populist radical right parties that predate the governmental cooperation. Consequently, many governmental policies on even populist radical right issues like immigration reflect at least as much the program of the mainstream right-wing party as that of the populist radical right one. Fifth, and finally, populist radical right parties prefer to keep 'one foot in and one foot out' of government, meaning that they prefer to keep their *oppositional image*, by using radical rhetoric and pushing for excessively radical policies, rather than run the risk of being perceived as a 'normal' governmental party and part of 'the corrupt elite' (see also Chapter 11).

So, all is well on the Western Front?

This all is not to say that populist radical right parties are destined to remain a relatively minor nuisance in West European democracies, although it is important to remember that in the past three decades the main threats to liberal democracy have come from the political mainstream rather than the political extremes – that is, Silvio Berlusconi in Italy, the Kaczyński brothers in Poland, and currently Viktor Orbán in Hungary (see Chapters 7 and 27), as well as from the anti-terror legislation after 9/11 (see Chapters 22–6). There are at least three reasons why populist radical right parties could become more influential in the (near) future.

First, partly because of their rise, but mostly because of the transformation of the mass media, we have seen a tabloidization of political discourse in the past decades. Tabloids and populist radical right parties share many similar attitudes and issues, which have come to dominate the political discourse in Europe in the past decades, providing at the very least a more favourable 'discursive opportunity structure' for populist radical right parties and their policies.

Second, the electoral trend of populist radical right parties is clearly up. Not only are there more successful parties today than 30 years ago, several have established themselves in their national political systems. And while the economic crisis has slowed down their electoral growth, by returning the political debate to socio-economic rather than socio-cultural issues, there are good reasons to believe that the post-crisis era could see a resurgence of populist radical right parties – for instance, growing political dissatisfaction and Euroscepticism (see Chapter 3).

Third, and finally, some of the successful populist radical right parties have grown up. They have learned from mistakes during their first brushes with power and have often gained more experience at the sub-national level. I disagree, then, with the dominant strain in the populism literature that argues that populist parties are destined for success in opposition and failure in government. Like social democratic parties before the Second World War, and Green parties in the 1990s, populist radical right parties can make the transformation from successful opposition party to effective governing party.

But even in the unlikely event that populist radical right parties become major players in West European politics, it is unlikely that this will lead to a fundamental transformation of the political system. After all, the populist radical right is not a normal pathology of European democracy, unrelated to its basic values, but rather a pathological normalcy, which strives for the radicalization of mainstream values.

Notes

1 Cas Mudde, 'Thirty Years of Populist Radical Right Politics in Western Europe: So What? The 2012 Stein Rokkan Lecture', *European Journal of Political Research*, Vol. 52, No. 1, 2013, pp. 1–19.
2 Michael Minkenberg, 'The Radical Right in Public Office: Agenda-Setting and Policy Effects', *West European Politics*, Vol. 24, No. 4, 2001, p. 21.

3 The myth of Weimar Europe

Since the start of the Great Recession, the US subprime mortgage market crash that turned into a global economic crisis, it has become received wisdom that the far right is on the rise. How else could it be? Since the rise of the Nazis in Weimar Germany conventional wisdom holds that economic crises breed far right success. While there is no really elaborate academic theory underlying it, the economic-crisis-breeds-extremism thesis might be one of the most popular social science theories out there today (together with the closely related modernization theory). It is received wisdom among academics, journalists and policy makers alike.

The idea that the Great Recession fuelled a resurgence of far right, i.e. both radical and extreme right parties, is based mostly on two highly publicized cases, both in 2012: the National Front (FN) in France and Golden Dawn in Greece. Having finally replaced her father, party founder Jean-Marie Le Pen, Marine Le Pen took the FN as a phoenix from her ashes. After years of electoral decline, she led the party to its best ever results in the presidential and second best ever results in the parliamentary election of 2012. Even more shocking were the two Greek parliamentary elections in May and June 2012, which saw the entrance of the, until then marginal, neo-Nazi Golden Dawn into the Greek parliament (see Chapter 19). While many radical right parties have entered national legislatures since 1980, this was the first time that an openly extreme right party was able to pull it off. For most observers, academic and non-academic, these two cases were symptomatic for the rise of the far right in Europe, the expected result of the economic crisis.

An analysis of the recent electoral results of far right parties in EU member states shows a very different picture, however. If we compare the pre-crisis (2005–8) with the crisis (2009–13) results, the striking *lack* of electoral success of the far right stands out most.[1] First of all, more than one quarter, eight of the twenty-eight, current EU member states have no far right party to speak of. Interestingly, this includes four of the five bailout countries

(Cyprus, Ireland, Portugal and Spain); Greece being the only exception! Second, among the twenty countries with (somewhat) relevant far right parties, the electoral results are almost evenly split: eleven have seen an increase in electoral support for far rights parties during the period 2005–13, and nine have not.[2] Third, of the eleven countries with rising far right support, only five saw more or less sizeable increases in absolute (rather than relative) terms. However, against these five countries, in which far right parties gained more than five per cent of the vote between 2005 and 2013, stand three countries that saw a *de*crease by more than five per cent (Belgium, Romania and Slovakia).

The five EU countries that have seen a substantial rise of populist radical right electoral support are Austria (+13.1 per cent), Finland (+14.9 per cent), France (+9.3 per cent), Hungary (+14.5 per cent) and Latvia (+6.9 per cent). Greece comes close (+4.7 per cent), almost doubling its support, and will be discussed separately below. The single biggest increase is in Finland, where the True Finns jumped from 4.1 per cent in 2007 to 19.0 per cent in 2011. Interestingly, Finland was among the least affected EU countries, having faced its own economic crisis over a decade before the Great Recession. This notwithstanding, the economic crisis played a major role in the electoral campaign and success of the True Finns (PS), which vehemently opposed the bailouts. That said, the populist radical right status of the party is heavily debated, and it seems at best a borderline case.

The other two West European countries, Austria and France, have both suffered rather moderate economic distress, unlike the two East European countries (Hungary and Latvia). And while there is no doubt that the parties have profited from political dissatisfaction related to the economic crisis, both the FN and the Austrian Freedom Party (FPÖ) are established populist radical right parties, which have gained similar electoral results well before the crisis started (in 1997 and 1999, respectively). This leaves Hungary and Latvia, two of the hardest-hit countries in the former East, which as a region has not born the brunt of the Great Recession.

The rise of the Movement for a Better Hungary (Jobbik) has received significant academic and public attention, although it sometimes takes a backseat to the troubling policies of Premier Viktor Orbán's Fidesz government (see Chapters 7 and 27). Jobbik won a staggering 16.7 per cent of the vote in its first elections in 2010, replacing the marginal Hungarian Justice and Life Party (MIÉP) as the country's premier populist radical right party. This was the second biggest increase after Finland. But where the True Finns might be too moderate to be considered populist radical right, Jobbik might be too extreme. It walks a fine line between radical right and extreme right, in part represented by the political party (Jobbik) and the paramilitary movement (Hungarian Guard). Although Hungary has been extremely hard hit by the economic crisis, and has been flirting with a bailout, the 2010 elections were not really fought over the Great Recession. While both Fidesz and Jobbik profited from widespread political dissatisfaction, the cause was partly economic (i.e. the economic crisis), partly political (i.e. the Gyurcsány scandal).

The most pure case of the economic crisis theory seems, oddly enough, the tiny and little noticed Baltic country of Latvia. Hit extremely hard by the banking crisis, the American Nobel laureate and economist Paul Krugman called Latvia 'the new Argentina' in the *New York Times* in 2008. The fact that the populist radical right National Alliance (NA) has practically doubled its electoral support between 2006 and 2011 should therefore surprise no one. Moreover, following the Weimar scenario even more perfectly, the NA joined the Latvian government in 2011, although as a junior coalition partner. The puzzling aspect is, however, that the rise of the NA took place in 2011, after the peak of the economic crisis. While the economy nosedived in 2008–9, the NA gained a mere 0.7 per cent in the 2010 elections (compared to 2006). Yet, after the economy stabilized in 2010, the party jumped from 7.7 to 13.9 per cent in the 2011 elections. That year, the Latvian economy showed a real GDP growth of 5.5 per cent!

In short, the numbers simply don't add up. Despite all the talk of the rise of the far right as a consequence of the Great Recession, the sober fact is that far right parties have gained support in only eleven of the twenty-eight EU member states (39 per cent), and increased their support substantially in a mere five (18 per cent). Just as was the case during the Great Depression, i.e. Weimar Germany (and to a lesser extent Italy), the unfounded generalization of a few high-profile cases (i.e. France and Greece) has obscured the fact that the vast majority of EU countries have electorally and politically marginal populist radical right parties, both before and during the Great Recession. At the end of 2013, only about half of EU member states have a populist radical right in their national parliament, and only two in their national government, as junior partners (Bulgaria and Latvia).

This is not to say that the far right is irrelevant in contemporary Europe, or that the situation in Greece is not extremely troubling. Rather, it is a warning against selective perception and sensationalist generalizations as well as a call for keeping our eye on the real political threats of today. Throughout Europe politicians use the alleged threat of a far right resurgence, backed by the economic crisis thesis, to push through illiberal policies. A relatively moderate example is Greek premier Antonis Samaras' increasing support for tough discourse on immigration and immigrants. An extreme example is Hungarian premier Viktor Orbán's frontal attack on the country's constitutional order. Both have defended their actions as necessary in the wake of mounting far right pressures, presenting their governments as the only realistic alternative to the far right hordes. And although both countries are indeed confronted with a particularly dangerous far right opposition, which is truly anti-democratic, neither party is even close to gaining political power.

In short, Europe is not at the brink of a Weimar Germany scenario (see also Chapter 19). In sharp contrast to the situation in Weimar Germany in the early 20th century, extremists are relatively minor political players in the Europe of the early 21st century. Even more importantly, whereas the Weimar Republic was a democracy without democrats, democracy is hegemonic in contemporary Europe. It is important that Europeans remain vigilant toward the far right, but they should not get paralyzed by an irrational fear, which can turn them into the uncritical masses of opportunistic and power-hungry 'democratic' political leaders.

Notes

1   In most cases the comparison is based on the vote share for a single party in each election; however, in certain cases the figure is an aggregate change based on more than one party. Figures taken from European Election Database (EED).

2   Note that this analysis includes two parties that in most of my later analyses are excluded, namely the True Finns in Finland and the National Alliance (NA) in Latvia. The True Finns, now Finns Party, are probably better categorized as right-wing populist, as nativism is not a core ideological value, while the NA is a coalition of two parties, the conservative For Fatherland and Freedom/LNNK and the populist radical right All for Latvia! (See also Chapter 4).

4   Putin's Trojan horses?

Five theses on Russia and the European far right

The news that the French National Front (FN) has received a nine million euro loan through a Kremlin-close Russian bank – are there any other? – has sent the international media into a speculation frenzy. The recent stories come on top of months of international media coverage about the alleged pro-Russian bias of European far right parties, which, not coincidentally, started in the run up to the 2014 European elections. But what is 'the' European far right's position on Russia? Are they ideological brethren or opportunistic collaborators? And is the far right really Putin's Trojan Horse in the European Union (EU), as the media wants us to believe?

There are many documented personal connections

Leaders of some of the most prominent far right parties in Europe have visited high-ranking Russian politicians over the past years. Already in May 2013, before the start of the Ukrainian crisis, Gábor Vona, leader of the Movement for a Better Hungary (Jobbik), gave a lecture at Lomonosov University in Moscow at the invitation of the notorious Russian far right 'Eurasianist' Alexander Dugin, then still a professor there. He also met with a host of high-ranking Duma members, mostly linked to the energy sector. A month earlier Marine Le Pen had met in Moscow with Sergei Naryshkin, speaker of the Duma, while Italian Northern League (LN) leader Matteo Salvini visited leaders of Putin's United Russia parliamentary faction in the Duma in October 2014. A month later a heavy Austrian Freedom Party (FPÖ) delegation visited Moscow, where party leader Heinz-Christian Strache participated in a roundtable on 'overcoming the crisis in Europe,' chaired by Russian Foreign Minister Sergei Lavrov.

In return, a prominent United Russia member, Viktor Zubarev, was present at an important meeting in Turin, Italy, where leading members of the Belgian Flemish Interest (VB), Dutch Party for Freedom (PVV), FN, FPÖ, and LN discussed the activities of the European Alliance for Freedom

(EAF), the now largely defunct EU-wide collaboration of far right parties (see Chapters 5 and 6). Last month Andrei Isayev, deputy chairman of the Duma, was the only non-far right foreign speaker at the FN party meeting in Lyon, where he toasted France and stressed the good relations between Moscow and the FN.

In addition, some far right politicians have functioned as referendum and election observers for the pro-Russian separatists in the so-called People's Republic of Donetsk and Luhansk, also known as *Novorossyia* (New Russia). As meticulously documented by the Ukrainian researcher Anton Shekhovtsov, the obscure Eurasian Observatory For Democracy & Elections (EODE) of marginal Belgian far right activist Luc Michel has organized observers for the (illegal) referendum in Crimea of March 2014 and the (illegal) elections in 'New Russia' of October 2014.[1] While the majority of observers that actually went were related to marginal far left and far right parties, some (prominent) members of Attack (Bulgaria), FN, FPÖ, Jobbik, and VB were also present.

There are few documented financial connections

Rumours about Russian financial support for EU far right parties are not new.[2] For instance, allegations of Jobbik being 'backed by Russian rubles' date back to at least 2010, yet no evidence has ever been presented. Similarly vague is the case of Béla Kovács (aka 'KGBéla'), a Jobbik Member of the European Parliament (MEP) alleged to be a spy for Russia.[3] Despite sensationalist stories in the Hungarian and international press, the evidence presented for the allegations does not go much beyond the facts that he has a Russian wife and holds a pro-Russian position. In an even weirder conspiracy theory, the far right Alliance of European National Movements (AENM), of which Kovács is a co-founder and current president, is accused of Russian financing. The EANM is a pan-European organization of mostly small far right parties, which used to include the strongly anti-Russian All-Ukrainian Union 'Svoboda' as an observer member.

The only documented financial connections between Russia and a far right party (so far) are related to the FN. In 2015 the party received a nine million euro 'loan' through a Russian bank, which Marine Le Pen has confirmed – she denies, however, that the real amount is in the order of 40 million euro – while her father has admitted a two million euro loan from 'a former KGB spy.' In both cases there is no evidence (yet) of a direct link to the Kremlin or of specific (political) expectations related to the loans. Allegations toward other far right parties have been strongly denied. For example, FPÖ leaders Strache and Harald Vilimsky have stated categorically that the party has received 'not a ruble' from Russia or any other foreign country.

Most far right parties are anti-EU rather than pro-Russia

The Hungarian think tank Political Capital has published the most comprehensive study of far right positions on Russia to date.[4] It concludes that 'most major European far-right parties typically fall in the 'committed' category, openly professing their sympathy for Russia.' However, the study includes 24 parties, of which many have never been relevant (e.g. Czech Workers' Party and Estonian Independence Party), are no longer relevant (e.g. Polish League of Families and Greater Romania Party), or are not far right (e.g. Lithuanian Order and Justice and Polish Self-Defence). Moreover, what constitutes a 'committed' (i.e. pro-Russian) position remains vague in the study, as is the case in most media coverage.

It would make sense to (only) speak of a 'pro-Russian' position when a party sees (Putin's) Russia in a positive light, representing core values that the far right party supports itself. If parties see Russia as a country like all others, they are 'neutral' – the difference between 'neutral' and 'open' in the study adds more confusion than clarification. Finally, a party is 'anti-Russian' when it considers Russia in a negative light, representing core values it opposes – this has become the default position within the EU today.

If we look only at the relevant far right parties within the EU, we find a (small) majority that is 'neutral,' a (large) minority that is pro-Russian, and virtually no far right party that is anti-Russian (see Table 4.1).[5] In fact, the only party that is anti-Russian, the Latvian National Alliance (NA), is a borderline case; it is a merger of two parties, All for Latvia! (VL) and For Fatherland and Freedom/LNNK (TB/LNNK), which are both strongly anti-Russian, but only the VL is far right – TB/LNNK is better classified as national conservative.

Five of the twelve (eleven if NA is excluded) far right parties are pro-Russian. These parties see Russia as a natural ally of their country in a world

Table 4.1 The position on Russia of 12 relevant far right parties

Pro-Russian	Neutral	Anti-Russian
Ataka	DF	NA
FN	HSP	
LN	FPÖ	
Jobbik	PVV	
XA	SD	
	VB	
5	6	1

dominated by Israel and the United States. For example, Golden Dawn (XA) declares itself 'a natural ally of Russia' in its fight against 'American expansionist policies,' while Jobbik leader Vona has stated that 'Euro-Atlantism must be replaced by Eurasianism,' a term used by both Dugin and Putin. Various far right politicians have heaped praise on Putin and Russia. For instance, Aymeric Chauprade, leader of the FN EP faction and Marine Le Pen's advisor on foreign policy, sees Russia as 'the hope of the world against new totalitarianism,' while Marine Le Pen allegedly has said that Putin is a defender of 'the Christian heritage of European civilization.'

Despite these strong public statements, mostly made in Russia and in the past two years, the official party literature entails a much more moderate position on Russia. Jobbik's 2010 election manifesto *Radical Change* only includes one reasonably neutral statement on Russia – 'We will develop a partner relationship with Russia, which should bring our homeland positive economic and national-political benefits' (p. 20) – while XA officially supports a Third Way, 'opposed both to communist internationalism and universalism-liberalism,' a position held by most extreme right – but few radical right (e.g. FN, FPÖ, VB) – parties during the Cold War. The LN has no mention to its position on Russia in its 2013 and 2014 programs, while the FN program *Our Project* (2014) just speaks of 'restarting the Franco–Russian cooperation' in the area of defence and of forming a 'trilateral alliance Paris–Berlin–Moscow' (note that Paris comes first).

Most relevant far right parties take a fairly neutral, if any, position on Russia. They hardly address the country or its leader in their official literature. For instance, the FPÖ devotes little attention to the relationship with Russia in its party programs. Even the extensive 'Handbook of Freedomite Politics' (2013) mainly notes, 'The Russian sphere of interest is to be respected to the extent that Russia respects Europe's sphere of interest' (p.270). Many parties almost exclusively deal with Russia in the context of EU policies. For example, the Sweden Democrats (SD) voted against the Ukraine Association Agreement in the European Parliament (EP), arguing that the Ukraine conflict is 'only the latest in a series of foreign policy failures' of the EU. Similarly, while PVV leader Geert Wilders echoes some of the standard Russian propaganda on Ukraine, such as virtually equating Euromaidan supporters with 'National Socialists, Jew-haters and other anti-democrats,' he has explicitly condemned Russia's interventions in Ukraine. And, while the Danish People's Party (DF) has recognized the (illegal) Crimea referendum, it has also proposed the use of Denmark's navy to send Russia a warning and let Poland and the Baltic states know that the country supports them.

In short, the positions of the EU's relevant far right parties are not so straightforwardly pro-Russian as the media have made them out to be.

A small majority of far right parties is neutral towards Russia, seeing it as a country like all others, and opposing a different treatment of it. A large minority is pro-Russian, seeing the country and its leader as a positive international force and a role model for its own country. In all cases the party position on Russia is very strongly related to the party position on the EU. In most cases it is indeed a *consequence* of their Euroscepticism.

There is nothing specifically 'Russian' about the relationship

Several commentators have likened Russian support for the EU's far right parties to Soviet support for West European communist parties during the Cold War. In the words of the American political scientist Mitchell Orenstein, 'Russia today is using a lot of the old Soviet techniques, but this time is finding the far right a better partner than the far left.'[6] But the connection between Russia and the far right is much weaker than that between the Soviet Union and the far left ever was. There is no far right Comintern or Cominform. The Kremlin doesn't control the far right parties and is not even looking for full control. In the self-flattering terms of FN foreign affairs spokesman Ludovic de Danne, 'Our independent stance is appreciated by those in power in Russia, that's why we have good contacts with them.'

In fact, Russia sees the far right largely the same as the Soviet Union and its satellites saw the far right in Western Europe during the Cold War, which it at times actively supported (particularly in West Germany). They are seen as a useful irritant within the EU, one of its main competitors, potentially obstructing (perceived) anti-Russian actions, and providing Russian elite with propagandistic ammunition for the home audience. In their propaganda, Russian elites alternate between references to the European far right as positive examples of 'the protection of genuine and social interests of the population' and negative examples of widespread xenophobia in the European Union.

In the end, Russia's support for Europe's far right is part of an age-old strategy of divide and conquer, which democracies and dictatorships all around the world have been practicing since time immemorial. Leaving aside institutionalized support that generally stays within the same ideological family – such as the massive support to East European parties by western party organizations like the German Friedrich Ebert Foundation (FES) or the US International Republican Institute (IRI). There are hundreds of historical and contemporary examples of more opportunistic western support for 'enemies of my enemy.' US Senator John McCain is making a new career out of photo ops with highly dubious politicians, including Oleg Tyahnybok, leader of the far right Ukrainian party Svoboda.

Far right parties are not Putin's real Trojan Horses

Finally, while the connections between the European far right and Russia deserve serious scrutiny, rather than wild speculation, they are not Putin's real Trojan Horse within the EU. Rather, they are the Greek soldiers throwing spears from outside Troy, slightly threatening and barely effective. Putin's real Trojan Horses are not to be found on Europe's political margins but in the EU's political mainstream. They include various establishment newspapers (including *Figaro* and *The Telegraph*), which publish the online supplement 'Russia Beyond the Headlines,' produced by *Rossiyskaya Gazeta*, the official newspaper of the Kremlin. They include the CEOs of major companies like Siemens and Total, who strongly oppose the Russian sanctions. They include former prime ministers of major EU countries, like Silvio Berlusconi, Tony Blair and Gerhard Schroeder, who still hold serious economic and political cloud. And, most of all, they include political leaders like Hungarian Prime Minister Viktor Orbán, who is worth more to Putin than all far right parties together.

Notes

1   Anton Shekhovtsov, 'Pro-Russian Extremists Observe the Illegitimate Crimean "Referendum"', *Voices of Ukraine*, 17 March 2014, available at http://maidan translations.com/2014/03/17/anton-shekhovtsov-pro-russian-extremists-observe-the-illegitimate-crimean-referendum/ (last visited 21 October 2015).
2   Mitchell A. Orenstein, 'Putin's Western Allies', *Foreign Affairs* (blog), 25 March 2014, available at https://foreignaffairs.com/articles/russia-fsu/2014-03-25/putins-western-allies (last visited 21 October 2015).
3   Mitchell A. Orenstein and Péter Krekó, 'A Russian Spy in Brussels?' *Foreign Affairs* (blog), 29 May 2014, available at https://foreignaffairs.com/articles/hungary/2014-05-29/russian-spy-brussels (last visited 21 October 2015).
4   Political Capital, 'The Russian Connection: The Spread of Pro-Russian Policies on the European Far Right' [working paper]. Budapest, Hungary: Political Capital Institute, 2014.
5   This includes all far right parties within the EU that currently hold representation in their national parliament or in the European Parliament (EP). The NPD has been excluded because its EP representation is based on less than 1 per cent of the German vote.
6   Quoted in Paul Ames, 'Europe's far right is embracing Putin', *Business Insider*, 10 April 2014, available at http://businessinsider.com/paul-ames-europes-far-right-is-embracing-putin-2014–4 (last visited 21 October 2015).

5   Local shocks

The far right in the 2014 European elections

'This is an earthquake': The far right rises as EU elections signal a massive shift across Europe.
   That 'earthquake' in Europe? It's far right gains in Parliament elections.[1]

The media headlines directly after the 2014 European elections had been written months before. The only real question was what the hyperbole of choice was going to be. In the end, 'earthquake' won. European elections have long been associated with the rise of far right parties, but 2014 was nevertheless special. For more than a year, European elites had warned of a huge electoral victory of 'Europe's populist insurgents' (*The Economist*), which the media loyally declared on the night of May 25, not even awaiting the full results. Pointing to the remarkable results in a few specific countries, *the* far right was declared the main winner of the 2014 European elections. This gave way to apocalyptic prophecies of the alleged dawn of a new Eurosceptic era.

   This essay analyses five aspects of the far right in the 2014 European elections. First, it gives a short overview of the pre-election period, discussing the far right campaign as well as the anti-far right media campaigns. Second, it presents the electoral results of far right parties and compares them to the 2009 European elections. Third, it analyzes the 2014 results in more detail, showing that the far right hardly broke new ground, and mainly succeeded in countries where it was already well established. Fourth, it examines the presence of the far right in the new European Parliament, highlighting the continuing failure of political group formation. And, fifth, I conclude with a short assessment of the main consequences of the far right's 'success.'

The pre-election period

The far right dominated the international media coverage in the run up to the European elections. Years before the elections were actually held, commentators were speculating about a rise in support for the far right. *Newsweek* already proclaimed 'The Rise of the Extreme Right' in September 2010, while most international media published similar stories in the next years. In 2012 the media were put into a real frenzy by the strong performance of (new) National Front (FN) leader Marine Le Pen in the French presidential elections and the surprising success of the neo-Nazi Golden Dawn (XA) in the Greek parliamentary elections (see Chapter 3). On top of that, the US government shutdown in 2013 led to warnings of a possible EU shutdown, as a consequence of the imminent success of 'Europe's Tea Parties' (*The Economist*) in the 2014 European elections.[2]

The far right added to these expectations with the new, and quite unexpected, political alliance between Marine Le Pen and Geert Wilders, leader (and only member) of the Dutch Party for Freedom (PVV). Wilders had always kept his distance from the FN, before arguing that the party was far right and anti-Semitic, but changed his position in light of the new FN leadership (his official reason) and his own party's electoral defeat and political marginalization in the Netherlands (the more probable real reason). In November 2013, Le Pen and Wilders announced that they would constitute a political group in the European Parliament, the European Alliance for Freedom (EAF).

While Euroscepticism was still the default far right position during the 2014 European elections, as it has been since at least the Maastricht Treaty of 1992, almost all parties had become more critical of the European Union (EU) as a consequence of the economic crisis in general, and the bailouts in particular. For the first time, several of the most successful parties were arguing for their country to leave the EU (e.g. FN and PVV). The other EAF members continued to call for reform rather than the out-right rejection of the EU, even though the implied reforms would amount to the rejection of the EU's core foundations.

The elections

As the media never tired of noting, far right parties increased their representation in the European Parliament (EP), gaining a record 51 MEPs, up 15 compared to the previous European elections of 2009 (see Table 5.1). The precise numbers depend on issues of conceptualization and categorization. Using a broad interpretation, the British anti-racist organization Hope Not Hate calculated that 16,835,421 Europeans (or 10.3 per cent) voted for

Table 5.1 European election results of main far right parties in votes and seats, 2014 and change (2014–2009)

Country	Far right party	Per centage of vote		Number of seats
		2014	Change	2014	Change
Austria	Austrian Freedom Party (FPÖ)	19.7	+7.0	4	+2
Belgium	Flemish Interest (VB)	4.1	−5.8	1	−1
Bulgaria	Ataka	3.0	−9.0	0	−2
Denmark	Danish People's Party (DF)	26.6	11.8	4	+2
France	National Front (FN)	25.0	18.7	24	+21
Germany	German National Democratic Party (NPD)	1.0	+1.0	1	+1
Greece	Popular Orthodox Rally (LAOS)	2.7	−4.5	0	−2
	Golden Dawn (XA)	9.4	+8.9	3	+3
Hungary	Movement for a Better Hungary (Jobbik)	14.7	−0.1	3	0
Italy	Northern League (LN)	6.2	−4.0	5	−4
Netherlands	Party for Freedom (PVV)	13.2	−3.8	4	−1
Romania	Greater Romania Party (PRM)	2.7	−6.0	0	−3
Slovakia	Slovak National Party (SNS)	3.6	−2.0	0	−1
Sweden	Sweden Democrats (SD)	9.7	+6.4	2	+2
United Kingdom	British National Party (BNP)	1.1	−4.9	0	−2
European Union		6.8	+0.8*	51	+15

* This is the average change in percentage for the 14 countries included here.

Source: www.results-elections2014.eu/en/election-results-2014.html

a far right party in the 2014 European elections.[3] This was over six million voters more than in 2009, or roughly 160 per cent of the 2009 far right electorate. Following my more narrow interpretation, 11,095,265 people (or 6.8 per cent) voted for far right parties.[4] This notwithstanding, it is clear that Europe as a whole wasn't hit by a far right earthquake.

As has been the case since the emergence of the so-called 'third wave' of far right parties in the early 1980s, the successes of individual parties differed significantly across the continent. For example, only ten of the twenty-eight member states elected far right MEPs (i.e. 36 per cent). Moreover, far right parties *gained* (additional) seats in just six countries, while they *lost* seats in seven others. Most striking of all, while two far right parties entered the European Parliament for the first time (SD and XA), five lost their representation altogether – Attack in Bulgaria, BNP in the UK, LAOS in Greece, PRM in Romania, and SNS in Slovakia.

In fact, in many ways the success of the European far right is largely the success of the FN. Its 4,711,339 voters account for 42.5 per cent of all far right voters in the 2014 European elections! Similarly, the increase in FN support, of 3,619,648 voters, constitutes roughly two-third of the new far right electorate. Not surprising then that the total increase of 15 far right MEPs, compared to the 2009 election, was almost exclusively because of the huge gains of the FN, which won an additional 21 seats, compensating for the various losses in other countries. The FN won almost half (41 per cent) of all far right seats in the European Parliament.

Analysing the 2014 far right results

One of the main problems with political analyses, both in academia and the media, is that they are obsessed with the alleged 'new,' at the expense of the often much more relevant 'old.' This holds particularly true for analyses of the far right, which has been proclaimed to be 'new' several times over since the emergence of the original 'new extreme right' in the early 1980s. So, what is actually new about the 2014 European elections?

First and foremost, for the first time in postwar history, far right parties have come first in nationwide elections in an EU member state. As expected, the FN topped the polls with 25 per cent of the vote, well ahead of the mainstream right-wing Union for a Popular Republic (UMP), with 20.8 per cent, and the mainstream left-wing Socialist Party (PS), with a mere 14 per cent. More surprising was the stunning victory of the DF, which gained 26.6 per cent of the Danish vote, leaving the mainstream left Social Democrats (S) and mainstream right Danish Liberal Party *Venstre* (V) well behind, with 19.1 and 16.8 per cent respectively.

Both of these cases are well-explained by the 'second-order theory' of elections, which argues that in elections that are not about the national government big parties lose, particularly those in government, and turnout is low.[5] This is especially the case when second-order elections come midway through the first-term election cycle, i.e. in between two national parliamentary elections, as was the case in Denmark and France. This notwithstanding, the DF won 165,231 votes more than in the 2011 parliamentary elections, while the FN attracted 1,182,966 more voters than in the 2012 parliamentary elections (though 1,710,087 *less* than in the 2012 presidential elections).

Interestingly, the two parties that registered the highest far right scores in recent parliamentary elections, the FPÖ and Jobbik, did not do that well in the European elections. After having gone head-to-head with the two big parties, the Austrian People's Party (ÖVP) and the Austrian Social Democratic Party (SPÖ), the FPÖ finished well behind them. Its 19.7 per cent was 7 per cent higher than its 2009 result, but 0.8% lower than the 2013 parliamentary election results. Even more striking was the result of Jobbik, whose 14.7 per cent was 0.1 per cent lower than the 2009 score and a striking 5.8 per cent lower than in the 2014 parliamentary elections the preceding month. These results are also in line with second-order election theory, which argues that European elections held shortly after national parliamentary elections are 'throw-away elections,' which benefit governing parties still enjoying a honeymoon period and hurt protest parties, because people vote with the heart rather than the boot.

The second new feature is the election of representatives of neo-Nazi parties – the German NPD and the Greek XA. Extreme right parties have been represented in the EP before, i.e. the Italian Social Movement (MSI) and its various splits, but not in its racist neo-Nazi variety. While the NPD only entered the EP because of a change of the electoral rules in Germany, the XA gained a staggering 9.4 per cent of the vote, despite the fact that the party is under investigation for being a criminal organization and its main leaders were imprisoned during the election campaign.

In contrast to these two new developments, the European elections mostly showed more of the same, both empirically and theoretically. I will focus particularly on three specific features: (1) the role of the economy; (2) the East–West divide; and (3) the importance of rebranding. All of these factors have been regularly mentioned by academic and non-academic commentators in media reports on the 2014 European elections, and have been addressed in academic research on the far right since the 1990s.

The idea that far right parties profit from an economic crisis has been around since Adolf Hitler's rise to power in Weimar Germany in the early-1930s. This notwithstanding, the thesis does not hold up under empirical scrutiny (see Chapter 3). This is true for both the Great Depression and the Great Recession, and was confirmed in the 2014 European elections. Most striking, only one of the 'bailed out' countries returned far right MEPs (Greece) – interestingly, in four of the five bailout countries, it was the far left that made (significant) gains. In fact, with the exception of Hungary, far right parties gained their highest scores almost exclusively in countries that were only little or moderately affected by the crisis, at least compared to other EU countries: Austria, Denmark, France, Netherlands and Sweden.

These results are fairly consistent with the rise of far right parties since the mid-1980s, at least in Western Europe. Not only did the parties emerge in a period of relative affluence, but they tend to perform best in the richer countries (e.g. Denmark, Switzerland) and regions (e.g. Flanders, Northern Italy). The explanation is that contemporary far right parties, just like Green parties, are mainly a post-materialist phenomenon, conducting identity politics and emphasizing socio-cultural issues. Economic issues are secondary for both the parties and their voters. Hence, in times of economic crisis, when socio-economic issues push socio-cultural issues to the sidelines, far right parties have less to offer and (some of) their voters will either not vote or look for a party with a more pronounced economic profile (and competence).

A much less noted development is the East-West divide in far right electoral success. Again, with the exception of Hungary, the far right lost its entire representation in the East. Supposedly, East Central Europe provides a fertile breeding ground for far right parties, including broadly shared prejudices towards minorities, high levels of corruption and a large reservoir of so-called 'losers of the transition.' One explanation for the abysmal performance of far right parties in East Central Europe is that mainstream (right-wing) parties in the region leave little space for the far right, given their nativist, authoritarian, and populist discourse. This is often mentioned as an explanation for the quick demise of the far right League of Polish Families (LPR), i.e. as a consequence of the right-wing turn of the conservative Law and Justice (PiS) party. However, in Hungary the at least equally authoritarian and nationalist Fidesz is confronted with the only strong far right party in the region, Jobbik (see Chapter 7). In this context, commentators argue that the relationship is actually the reverse, in that a very right-wing mainstream party legitimizes the far right, which helps them gain support.

Within the West European context I have called this the 'Chirac–Thatcher debate' and suggested that both arguments can be true. The missing piece in the puzzle is an intervening variable: issue ownership (see Chapter 1). If a far right party is able to 'own' far right issues like crime, corruption, and 'ethnic minorities,' it will profit from the rise in salience of that issue as a consequence of the discourse of the mainstream (right-wing) party. If it does not, the mainstream (right-wing) party can occupy the unclaimed issue and *own* it, leaving little space for the far right. What sets Eastern Europe apart from Western Europe is the lack of institutionalized parties and a stable party system, which also means that few parties, mainstream or far right, can establish let alone hold onto issue ownership.

Finally, a lot of commentators have explained the success of the far right in general, and the FN in particular, by arguing that they have rebranded, making their ideologies more moderate and their parties more professional. It is this alleged 'far right 2.0' that succeeded where the (presumably) 'far right 1.0' of anti-Semitic leaders and racist skinhead supporters failed. The thesis of a 'new radical right' is actually quite old and has been used several times since the early 1980s. Whereas Marine's father Jean-Marie Le Pen has become a caricature of himself in recent years, 25 years ago he was considered one of the most charismatic political leaders in Europe. Similarly, current FPÖ-leader Heinz-Christian Strache, or 'HC' as the party's cult of personality would have it, is heralded as part of 'a new generation of leaders' that looks much more respectable than the 'historic leaders' of the 1980s and 1990s. But journalists wrote exactly the same about his predecessor, Jörg Haider, for whom the term 'designer Fascist' was invented.

The far right in the European Parliament

National parliamentary elections are important for the constitution of both the parliament and the government. This is not the case in the EU, where the European Commission, and to a certain extent the European Council, constitute the 'government.' The post-election period in the European Parliament is instead dominated by the formation of political groups. To be officially recognized, a political group requires 25 members from at least one quarter of the member states (seven in the current legislature). Most committee positions, funding, and speaking time is divided on the basis of political groups, which leaves the non-affiliated MEPs, the so-called *Non-Inscrits* (NI), quite isolated and powerless.

At first sight, the far right should not have experienced any problems in forming a political group. It has 51 seats from ten member states. However, political group formation is determined by both ideological and strategic considerations. Simply speaking, ideologically there is a divide between extreme right and radical right parties, while strategically there is a division between nationally accepted and ostracized parties. This, together with conflicting nationalisms and personalities, makes far right collaboration in Europe problematic, as can be seen from their poor track record (see Chapter 6).

In the previous legislature, far right parties were divided between the Europe for Freedom and Democracy (EFD) political group and the NI. After frantic negotiations within the broader right-wing Eurosceptic camp, involving the 'soft Eurosceptic' European Conservatives and Reformists (ECR) as well as the 'hard Eurosceptic' EAF and EFD, the far right has become even more dispersed (see Chapter 16). First of all, the EFD lost its old far right members – the DF joined the ECR, the LN the EAF, and the SNS lost its representation – but gained a new one, the SD. Second, the FN, FPÖ, PVV, and VB have so far been unable to constitute the EAF, and remain temporarily in the NI. Finally, the more extreme parties (Jobbik, NPD, XA) are considered beyond the pale for all three groups and will probably stay in the NI for the duration of this legislative term.

Conclusion

The 2014 European elections were not a 'political earthquake' as a consequence of massive far right gains, as the international media so eagerly publicized. At best, they brought some local shocks, mostly caused by well-established far right parties that have been operating in a 'new' style for decades. Similarly, the much-hyped European Alliance for Freedom (EAF) confirmed the historical pattern of European collaboration between far right parties: fragmented and largely restricted to the usual suspects. Consequently, despite the media hype, the European elections have hardly changed the position of the far right within European politics.

Far right parties remain marginalized within the EU power structure, lacking individual representation in the European Council and European Commission, and group representation in the European Parliament. In fact, within the EP, the Europhile political groups continue to control all chairperson positions of the powerful parliamentary committees, excluding all Eurosceptic groups. Moreover, the far right lost influence in the only hard Eurosceptic group, as Europe for Freedom (EFD) transformed into Europe for Freedom and Direct Democracy (EFDD), replacing several far right parties with the idiosyncratic Italian populist Five Star Movement (M5S) of Beppe Grillo (see also Chapter 16).

Perhaps there has been a small effect on the political discourse, as the alleged rise of the far right has further helped to mainstream soft Euroscepticism. When the Dutch conservative-liberal Premier Mark Rutte remarks that 'the EU has to go back to its core,' and the German Social Democratic Party leader Sigmar Gabriel states that 'Europe is an elite project, too remote from the citizens,' soft Euroscepticism has truly arrived in the European political mainstream. Obviously, the transformation of the EU itself, as well as other factors like the economic crisis and the bailouts, play a much more important role in the mainstreaming of soft Euroscepticism than the alleged rise of the far Right. But the electoral pressure from hard Eurosceptic parties, most notably of the far right, has given mainstream leaders both cover and incentives to adopt soft Eurosceptic rhetoric (rather than policies).

However, the alleged rise of the far right has also helped discredit hard Eurosceptic arguments, ranging from a fundamental reform of the EU to national exit options (see part III). Rather than having to engage in a fundamental debate on these arguments, Europhile and soft Eurosceptic politicians can reject these arguments by linking them to the far right. For the best result, a reference to Golden Dawn will end any debate. While the far right straw man is certainly not new to the European debate, it has become increasingly important in a soft Eurosceptic world. Whereas before *any* critique of the EU could be disqualified as Eurosceptic, which was generally perceived to be bad and outside of the political mainstream, the boundaries are much less clear now. But one thing remains clear to all: if there is a link to neo-Nazis like Golden Dawn, it is bad!

Notes

1 The quotes are from *Associated Press* (26 May 2014) and *CNN* (26 May 2014), respectively.
2 See Cas Mudde, 'A European Shutdown? The 2014 European Elections and the Great Recession', *Washington Post*, 4 November 2013, available at: https://washingtonpost.com/news/monkey-cage/wp/2013/11/04/a-european-shutdown-the-2014-european-elections-and-the-great-recession/ (last visited 6 November 2015).
3 Hope Not Hate, 'Euro-vote Epic Over Bar the Shouting', available at: http://hopenothate.org.uk/2014/europe (last visited 21 October 2015).
4 This difference is mostly caused by my exclusion of the British UKIP, Finnish PS, Latvian NA and the Polish Congress of the New Right (KNP), which do not share *the combination of* nativism, authoritarianism and populism as their core ideological values. For a full discussion of my used terminology, see Cas Mudde, *Populist Radical Right Parties in Europe*. Cambridge: Cambridge University Press, 2007, Chapter 1.
5 For the original thesis, see Karlheinz Reiff and Hermann Schmitt, 'Nine Second-Order National Elections – A Conceptual Framework for the Analysis of European Elections Results', *European Journal of Political Research*, Vol. 8, 1990, pp. 3–44. A more recent application is Hermann Schmitt, 'The European Parliament Elections of June 2004: Still Second-Order?', *West European Politics*, Vol. 28, No. 3, 2005, pp. 650–79.

6   Europe of Nations and Freedoms

Financial success, political failure

Although Marine Le Pen and Geert Wilders made their usual bombastic statements, they rang more hollow than usual, even for most of the European media, which hardly ever misses an opportunity to proclaim the latest 'rise of the far right.' Le Pen, leader of the French National Front (FN), declared with populist pathos, 'We're here for our peoples, for their freedoms,' while Geert Wilders, leader of the Dutch Party for Freedom (PVV), added his usual combative streak, proclaiming, 'Today it's D-Day, we are at the beginning of our liberation.'

The main newsworthy aspect of today's launch of the far right political group Europe of Nations and Freedom (ENF in English, ENL in French) is that this time it seems to be actually happening. In the run-up to the European elections of May 2014 Le Pen and Wilders claimed for months that they had the members (see Chapter 5), but in the end had to admit that no one had joined their original core group of five, i.e. FN, PVV, Austrian Freedom Party (FPÖ), Flemish Block (VB) from Belgium, and Northern League (LN) from Italy. They announced they would have a group 'very soon,' which turned out to be over a year.

As expected, Le Pen and Wilders had to build their new group on the services of renegades of parties, rather than the parties themselves (see Table 6.1). Janice Atkinson was considered too corrupt for the United Kingdom Independence Party (UKIP) and its Europe for Freedom and Direct Democracy (EFDD) group, and will claim her expenses from the ENF in the future, while the two Polish members, Michal Marusik and Stanisław Żółtek, are hailed as 'the new moderate political leadership' of the Polish Congress for a New Right (KNP), a leader-centric party that recently ousted its leader Janusz Korwin-Mikke, its only popular politician. Hardly the basis of 'a real politically coherent EU-critical group,' as FPÖ General Secretary and European Parliament (EP) faction leader Harald Vilimsky made it out to be.

Table 6.1 Members of the 'Europe of Nations and Freedoms' (ENF) political group

Marine LE PEN	FN	1st Co-President
Marcel de GRAAFF	PVV	2nd Co-President
Harald VILIMSKY	FPÖ	Vice-President
Matteo SALVINI	LN	Vice-President
Michał MARUSIK	KNP	Vice-President
Janice ATKINSON	IND	Vice-President
Gerolf ANNEMANS	VB	Treasurer
Barbara KAPPEL	FPÖ	Member
Georg MAYER	FPÖ	Member
Franz OBERMAYR	FPÖ	Member
Louis ALIOT	FN	Member
Marie-Christine ARNAUTU	FN	Member
Nicolas BAY	FN	Member
Dominique BILDE	FN	Member
Marie-Christine BOUTONNET	FN	Member
Steeve BRIOIS	FN	Member
Mireille D'ORNANO	FN	Member
Edouard FERRAND	FN	Member
Sylvie GODDYN	FN	Member
Jean-François JALKH	FN	Member
Philippe LOISEAU	FN	Member
Dominique MARTIN	FN	Member
Joëlle MÉLIN	FN	Member
Bernard MONOT	FN	Member
Sophie MONTEL	FN	Member
Florian PHILIPPOT	FN	Member
Mylène TROSZCZYNSKI	FN	Member
Gilles LEBRETON	FN/RBM	Member
Jean-Luc SCHAFFHAUSER	RBM*	Member
Mara BIZZOTTO	LN	Member
Mario BORGHEZIO	LN	Member
Gianluca BUONANNO	LN	Member
Lorenzo FONTANA	LN	Member
Vicky MAEIJER	PVV	Member
Olaf STUGER	PVV	Member
Stanisław ŻÓŁTEK	KNP	Member

* RBM = Marine Blue Gathering, a group of far right and right individuals created by Marine Le Pen, which functions as part of FN faction within EP.

According to the press communiqué of the Directorate General of the President of the European Parliament of 24 June 2015, the ENF group has 36 MEPs from seven EU member states. More than half (19) are from Le Pen's FN, which dominates the far right within the EP (see Chapter 5), five come from the Italian LN, four each from the FPÖ and PVV, 2 from the KNP, 1 from VB, and 1 is independent. Ironically, at this moment the ENF has fewer MEPs than the five core parties had on the night of the European elections, as FN directly lost one MEP, Joëlle Bergeron, and recently expelled its founder, and Marine's father, Jean-Marie Le Pen. In solidarity, his long-time fellow-MEP Bruno Gollnisch will also stay out of the ENF. That leaves one missing FN MEP, Aymeric Chauprade, who is currently believed to be in Fuji. Chauprade was supposed to lead the new group, but fell out of favour with the Marine Le Pen in-crowd, and is now largely isolated (although he did join the ENF).

Let's be absolutely clear, the ENF is a financial success, but a political failure. It is estimated that the new political group will be able to get its hands on up to € 17.5 million in the next four years. This money is crucial for parties that are allegedly so cash-strapped that they have to borrow money from Putin's cronies in Russia (see Chapter 4). It will also create the necessary paid positions to distribute the patronage that keeps any party going – particularly for the FN, which has few MPs in the French parliament, as a consequence of the country's highly disproportional electoral system. While it will also give the parties a slightly larger presence within the EP, notably through some more speaking time, the ENF will be as isolated as the EFDD.

Politically the ENF is without any doubt a failure. Even one year after the European elections, with the British and Swedish elections over, Le Pen and Wilders have not been able to convince any of the preferred parties to join. The Czech Party of Free Citizens (*Svobodní*), Lithuanian Order and Justice (TT), and the Sweden Democrats (SD) remain within EFDD, while the Danish People's Party (DF) and the Finns Party (PS) enjoy the respectable cover of the European Conservatives and Reformists (ECR). Even the Polish KNP is divided over the EFDD, ENF, and *Non Inscrits* (non-attached, NI). Moreover, the party already had an uncertain future with its former leader Korwin-Mikke and seems destined for political oblivion without him.[1]

It is delightfully ironic that the creation of the anti-EU ENF was a perfect example of everything ENF politicians claim to despise about the EU. They bent the rules to be able to eat from the much-maligned EU troth and they did so by recruiting the stereotypical MEP, whose assistant was caught inflating her expenses claim. An opportunism shared by all political groups in the EU; from the centre-right European People's Party (EPP), which continue to support the self-proclaimed 'illiberal democrat' Hungarian premier Viktor Orbán (see Chapter 7), to the Progressive Alliance of Socialists & Democrats (S&D), which just re-elected the allegedly corrupt Bulgarian ex-premier Sergei Stanichev as president, and from the Europhile Alliance of Liberals and Democrats (ALDE), which harbors the corrupt

Bulgarian Movement for Rights and Freedom (MRF), to the Eurosceptic ECR, which attacks the UKIP-led EFDD as 'far right' but accepted the far right DF into its midst.

Note

1   And, indeed, Korwin-Mikke's new party, the Coalition for Renewal of the Republic – Liberty and Hope (KORWiN), did much better in the Polish parliamentary elections of October 2015 than the KNP, 4.8 and 0.03 per cent respectively, but the electoral threshold kept both out of the Sejm.

7   Viktor Orbán and the difference between radical right politics and parties

Last month Viktor Orbán gave the most significant radical right speech in Europe of the past decades.[1] To those unfamiliar with European politics this statement might not mean much, while those more or less familiar with European politics might be confused by it. After all, Orbán is the Prime Minister of Hungary and the leader of the Fidesz-Hungarian Civic Alliance , a party not considered 'radical right' by the vast majority of academics and pundits. In fact, this label is almost exclusively used for another party in the country, the Movement for a Better Hungary (Jobbik).

Orbán's speech raises several important questions about some basic political science insights into political parties in general, and radical right parties and politicians in particular. First, how are parties best classified cross-nationally? Second, what makes a political party radical right? And, third, are radical right politics limited to radical right parties?

What is a party family?

Let's start with the first issue, i.e. the cross-national categorization of political parties. Both in the academic and public debate political parties are categorized cross-nationally through the concept of the 'party family.' While few people have heard about party families, many people have used the concept in their discussions of (European) politics. Party families are cross-national groups of similar parties, such as Christian democratic parties, communist parties, Green parties, and radical right parties. Despite the popularity of the concept, however unconsciously, there is little academic debate about how best to define party families, on the one hand, and classify individual parties, on the other.

Six criteria are most often used to define party families.[2] I'll discuss their general strengths and weaknesses with particular reference to the case of Fidesz. The first criterion is *origins* of a party, i.e. under which historical circumstances did it emerge? The advantage of this criterion is that the origins of a party tend to be relatively easy to discern and they are constant. But that rigidity is also its main disadvantage, as some parties change, while their origins do not. Fidesz is a perfect example of this: founded as the Alliance of Young Democrats (Fidesz) in 1988, it was a youthful, libertarian, anti-communist party that opposed the fading Hungarian communist regime. But Fidesz has undergone many transformations since then, in terms of ideology, personnel, and organization – though not leaders! In fact, if Fidesz would not have changed fundamentally, Orbán could not be its leader today – he is 52 and Fidesz originally limited membership to people 35 and under.

The second, related, criterion is *sociology*, the socio-economic character-istics of a party's electorate. Sociology was in particular used to define the big mass parties of the early 20th century; socialist parties were the parties of the workers, Christian (democratic) parties of the religious, agrarian parties of the farmers, etcetera. Today, societies in western democracies have much less pronounced socio-economic distinctions: farmers and workers constitute small minorities, mostly ignored by the main parties, while secularization has marginalized the importance of the religious electorate (outside of a few countries like Poland and the United States). These trends are even more pronounced in post-communist Europe, where the middle class has only started to emerge in the past two decades. But the sociology of party electorates changes not only because of larger societal changes, but also because of changes in the parties themselves. Again, Fidesz is a perfect example. Its initial electorate consisted mainly of higher educated, urban, young voters, reflecting the party's mission. Today this group is only a small part of the Fidesz electorate, which consists increasingly of the lower educated, non-urban, working class.

The third criterion is party *name*. The assumption underlying it is: who better to classify a party than the party itself? And it works pretty well for many of the most important political parties in Europe. Just think of the Austrian Social Democratic Party (SPÖ), The Greens in Germany, the Christian Democratic Appeal (CDA) in the Netherlands, or the Conservative Party in the UK. Unfortunately, party names can be ambiguous, idiosyn-cratic, and even deceiving, particularly on the (far) right. For example, what do party names like Attack (Bulgaria), Unity (Latvia), Soldiers of Destiny (Fianna Fáil, Ireland), or We Can (Podemos, Spain) tell us about a party? Or what about the (now defunct) Dutch Center Party (CP) and the Liberal Democratic Party of Russia (LDPR), both parties with a radical right ideology? Fidesz' full name also sends mixed messages: Hungarian Civic Party-Alliance of Young Democrats points mostly to the right, but it is not exactly clear where on the broader right-wing spectrum.

A fourth criterion is *transnational federation*, i.e. the official international links that political parties establish. Again, the idea is that parties know best and that like likes like. There are some global party federations, like the Liberal International, but most are regional, such as the Federation of Green Parties in the Americas. Within Europe membership in the political groups and parties of the European Union (EU) are the most common basis for party classification. Traditionally the political groups in the European Parliament (EP) were relatively homogenous, in part a reflection of the larger homogeneity of countries in the smaller European (Economic) Community. Today all eight official political groups in the EP are a combination of ideological affinity and opportunistic power politics. Fidesz is part of the most powerful political group in the EU, the European People's Party (EPP), initially a group of centrist Christian democratic parties, hardly the (current) profile of Fidesz.

The fifth criterion is *policies* and gets closer to the core of what political parties say and do. One of the main problems with this criterion is, which policies do you focus on: those *proclaimed* in the party manifestos, those *proposed* in parliament, or those *implemented* in government? For some parties you only have manifestos, as they are not represented in parliament, while most parliamentary parties are not in government. There is often quite a significant difference between the policies parties proclaimed in their manifesto and those they implement in government. This is particularly the case in Europe, where most governments are coalitions of parties, which make policies on the basis of compromises between the different coalition members. But even in the rare occasions of single party governments, as has been the case in Hungary since Orbán came back to power in 2010, there can be big differences between proclaimed and implemented policies.[3] For example, few of the controversial, sweeping changes that Orbán introduced in the new Hungarian constitution of 2011 had been explicitly part of the Fidesz election manifesto for the 2010 elections.[4]

Which brings us to the sixth, and last, criterion: party *ideology*. While the most common descriptions of party families are clearly reflecting party ideology, i.e. Christian democratic parties and Green parties, the criterion of ideology is not without problems. Leaving aside theoretical debates about the definition and relevance of ideology, there are important questions about the correct operationalization and methodology of measuring ideology. Which data and which methods should we use?

The still dominant Comparative Manifestos Project (CMP) exclusively uses election manifestos and mainly scores quasi-sentences on the basis of ideological constructs (such as 'military: positive,' 'free market economy' and 'multiculturalism: negative'). The Chapel Hill Expert Survey (CHES) surveys political scientists, who are considered to be experts on political parties in a specific country, and asks them to score the position of the parties on several issues as well as the salience of that issue for the party (such as 'role of religious principles in politics' or 'importance/salience of cosmopolitanism vs. nationalism').

Both approaches have their own pros and cons. The CMP is limited to election manifestos, which have a specific function (i.e. attract voters) and are known to exaggerate the importance of popular issues and disregard more controversial issues. The CHES is more a peer survey than a true expert study, which selects a group of political scientists per country, and then by and large assumes that all are equally knowledgeable about all aspects of all parties. As few political scientists actually study party ideology, of any party, their classifications often reflect at least as much received wisdom as expert knowledge, particularly about smaller and non-mainstream parties. That said, the alternative, an in-depth, mixed-method analysis of a broad range of literature of political parties across Europe, would require phenomenal resources, which means that CMP and CHES are the best available data for broad, cross-national studies of party ideologies.

Is Fidesz a radical right party?

As is the case with most political parties, there are few studies of the party ideology of Fidesz. There are even fewer *systematic* studies of its party ideology, i.e. employing qualitative or quantitative methods to analyze a broad range of official party sources – including internally oriented sources, like party papers. In now somewhat dated studies of the early 2000s Fidesz is classified as 'conservative' and 'centre-right.'[5] More recently, Hungarian political scientist András Bozóki has gone a step further, writing that Fidesz has created 'a Hungarian version of the New Right, a mixture of populism, conservatism, and plebeian, redistributionist, economic nationalism.'[6] The most recent classifications by the comparative studies discussed above come to fairly similar conclusions. CMP classifies Fidesz as a 'conservative' party, while CHES considers the party right-wing but not far right (yet) – its score is 7.9 on a 10-point scale, while Jobbik is placed at 9.7.

Yet, over the past years Orbán has made many high-profile statements, some followed by controversial actions, that go well beyond conservatism, as understood within contemporary Europe. After undermining key features of liberal democracy in Hungary, mostly but not exclusively through the new constitution, he declared in the summer of 2014 that 'liberal democratic states can't remain globally competitive' and openly acknowledged that he wants to transform Hungary into an 'illiberal democracy.'

In 2015 he radicalized further, calling for the reintroduction of the death penalty and recommending internment camps for illegal immigrants. And then there was the speech[7] at the 26th Bálványos summer open university and student camp last month, in which Orbán said:

In other words, what is at stake today is Europe and the European way of life, the survival or extinction of European values and nations – or, to be more precise, their transformation beyond all recognition. The question now is not merely what kind of Europe we Hungarians would like to live in, but whether Europe as we now know it will survive at all. Our answer is clear: we would like Europe to remain the continent of Europeans. This is what we would like. We only say 'we would like this', because this also depends on what others want. But there is also something which we not only would like, but which we want. We can say we want it, because it depends only on us: we want to preserve Hungary as a Hungarian country.

The fact that the vast majority of experts and journalists continue to classify Fidesz as a conservative rather than a radical right party, is undoubtedly influenced by the often multi-faceted interpretation of party families. As the party originated within the democratic mainstream, has a liberal-conservative party name, and is firmly entrenched in centre-right transnational party federations. Its electorate is more similar to centre-right than radical right parties – the latter attract an older, more masculine, and predominantly working class support. Finally, in its official election manifestos Fidesz largely steers clear of openly radical right policies and statements.

Moreover, many commentators argue that Orbán uses radical right statements for electoral purposes, i.e. to occupy the space left by the implosion of the Hungarian Democratic Forum (MDF) in the 1990s and to fight off competition from the radical right Jobbik today. But can a party really be 'just strategic' for most of its existence? And does it still matter whether Fidesz *is* a radical right party or a party that *uses* radical right policies and rhetoric? The answer is, as so often, yes and no.

Radical right politics versus radical right parties

The difference between the radical right as an ideology and as a strategy can be illustrated with a Hungarian example: will Hungary change fundamentally if Jobbik rather than Fidesz would be in power? Only a true cynic would answer 'no' to this. Irrespective of whether Jobbik is currently campaigning with a more moderate image than Fidesz, there is no doubt that Jobbik would implement some fundamentally different policies in key areas. Among others, Jobbik would almost certainly (try to) pull Hungary out of the EU, rather than just criticize it, and align it more openly with Putin's Russia. It would also seriously undermine the rights of minorities in Hungary, most notably Jews and Roma. Still, despite the fact that Jobbik is a radical right party and Fidesz is possibly not, there are three important reasons why Fidesz is a bigger radical right threat than Jobbik.

First, radical right *politics* are not limited to radical right *parties*. Just like (nominally) social democratic parties and politicians can implement neoliberal policies, just think of Bill Clinton and Tony Blair, conservative (and other) parties can propose and even introduce (populist) radical right policies, i.e. policies informed by nativism, authoritarianism, and populism (see Chapter 1). Think about the anti-immigration policies proposed and implemented by prime ministers John Howard and Tony Abbott of the centre-right Liberal Party of Australia, the anti-Sharia legislation adopted by (mostly) Republican Party dominated legislatures in more than twenty US states, or the cross-party support for authoritarian counter-terrorism measures throughout western democracies in the aftermath of the terrorist attacks of 9/11.

Second, while Jobbik is a more (genuinely) radical right than Fidesz, Jobbik is in opposition and Fidesz is in power. In fact, only very few governments in western democracies include radical right parties and in most that do the radical right party is almost always a junior party (see Chapter 2). Moreover, academic research has shown that radical right parties tend to be relatively ineffective in government – though that could chance in time when they gain more experience. One of the main reasons for their modest impact is that radical right parties, unlike their mainstream counterparts, lack national and international supporters, which brings us to the third and final point.

Mainstream parties like Fidesz have the possibility to be more harmful for liberal democracy than radical right parties like Jobbik, because they often have the experience, power, skills, and (national and international) backing to implement illiberal policies. In the specific case of Fidesz, the effectiveness was increased significantly by the supermajority the party enjoyed until recently in the mono-cameral legislature. Most importantly, this allowed them to make constitutional changes by themselves.

But mainstream parties also tend to have supporters in important political positions within their own country, such as within the bureaucracy and judiciary, and outside of it. In fact, the key reason that Orbán can get away with policies that are much worse than those other politicians before him – like Vladimír Mečiar in Slovakia or the Kaczyński brothers in Poland (both in coalition with a radical right party during the height of the critique) – have been scolded and punished for, is that he has friends in powerful places. And none is more powerful than the EPP, the dominant political group in the EU, of which Orbán was one of the vice-presidents from 2002 until 2012. Even after all the controversial policies and statements of the past years, EPP president Joseph Daul recently said: 'Orbán is the "enfant terrible" of the

EPP family, but I like him.' And 'thus' the EPP continues to frustrate any EU attempts to sanction Hungary, despite it being in flagrant violation of several EU regulations.

Some broader lessons

While the situation of Fidesz and Hungary is extreme and unique, at least for the moment, there are broader lessons to draw from it for everyone academically or politically concerned with liberal democracy.

First, while we should remain vigilant of the radical right, and the more violent extreme right (like Golden Dawn in Greece or neo-Nazi groups like the National Socialist Underground in Germany), we should not be blinded by it. The vast majority of these groups have at best indirect power, which makes them dependent upon mainstream political actors to implement their policies.

Second, because they hold almost all political power in western democracies, mainstream parties are responsible for almost all of the illiberal policies. Even if they do this to fight of a (perceived) radical right challenger, like Fidesz claims, it is still the mainstream party that makes the decision to implement illiberal policies rather than try to fend of the electoral challenge with liberal democratic policies.

Third, although political parties are best classified on the basis of their party ideology, as expressed in both externally and internally oriented party literature, parliamentary and governmental parties should also be judged on what they *do*, rather than only on what they say. If a political party offers a conservative ideology in its literature, but proposes and implements radical right policies in parliament and government, it is probably better classified as a radical right party.

Fourth, and final, liberal democracies are threatened by illiberal parties, by mainstream parties implementing (for whatever reason) illiberal policies, and by the domestic and foreign actors that enable them (see also Chapter 27). In the case of Fidesz, far less damage would have been done to liberal democracy in Hungary if the EPP wouldn't have shielded the Orbán government from EU sanctions.

Notes

1   On the speech, see Cas Mudde, 'The Hungary PM Made a 'Rivers of Blood' Speech ... And No One Cares', *The Guardian*, 30 July 2015, available at http://theguardian.com/commentisfree/2015/jul/30/viktor-orban-fidesz-hungary-prime-minister-europe-neo-nazi (last visited 21 October 2015).
2   For a more elaborate discussion, see Peter Mair and Cas Mudde, 'The Party Family and Its Study', *Annual Review of Political Science*, Vol. 1, 1998, pp. 211–29.

3   Technically Fidesz is in a coalition with the Christian Democratic People's Party (KDNP), but that party is really a satellite of Fidesz.
4   On the new Hungarian constitution, see the various posts of Kim Lane Sheppele on Paul Krugman's *New York Times* blog 'The Conscience of a Liberal,' most notably 'Constitutional Revenge' (1 March 2013), available at http://krugman.blogs.nytimes.com/2013/03/01/guest-post-constitutional-revenge/?_r=1 (last visited 21 October 2015). See also the three articles on Hungary in *Journal of Democracy*, Vol. 23, No. 3, 2013.
5   See, respectively, Celia Kiss, 'From Liberalism to Conservatism: The Federation of Young Democrats in Post-communist Hungary', *East European Politics and Societies*, Vol. 16, No. 3, 2003, pp. 739–63; Brigid Fowler, 'Concentrated Orange: Fidesz and the Remaking of the Hungarian Centre-Right, 1994–2002', *Journal of Communist Studies and Transition Politics*, Vol. 20, No. 3, 2004, pp. 80–115.
6   András Bozóki, 'Consolidation or Second Revolution? The Emergence of the New Right in Hungary', *Journal of Communist Studies and Transition Politics*, Vol. 24, No. 2, 2008, pp. 191–231.
7   'Prime Minister Viktor Orbán's presentation at the 26th Bálványos Summer Open University and Student Camp', available at http://miniszterelnok.hu/in_english_article/prime_minister_viktor_orban_s_presentation_at_the_26th_balvanyos_summer_open_university_and_student_camp (last visited 21 October 2015).

Part II
Populism

8   Jean-Claude Juncker and the populist zeitgeist in European politics

The rise of populist parties is a hotly debated topic in European politics. It has become a rite of passage of national and European leaders to warn for their rise and the new President of the European Commission (EC), the former Luxembourg Prime Minister Jean-Claude Juncker, has not disappointed (see also Chapter 13). Already before the European elections of May 2014, eagerly anticipating his new position, he called upon Europeans to 'reject populism.' And in December 2014, in an interview with the Dutch daily *De Volkskrant*, he went a step further, accusing mainstream parties of 'imitating' populist parties. With his usual pathos he said, 'If the established parties continue to follow the populist parties, European countries will become ungovernable.'

Obviously, these remarks have to be taken with a grain of salt, as they come from an embattled politician. Juncker has had a rocky start to his first term as President of the European Commission, often seen as the 'government' of the European Union (EU). Within months he came under huge pressure, mostly from populist parties in the European Parliament (EP), because of the so-called 'Luxembourg Leaks', which uncovered secret tax deals between the Luxembourg government (under his leadership) and 350 major companies around the world. This all notwithstanding, the claim that mainstream parties are 'imitating' populist parties, particularly those of the populist radical right, has been around for a long time.

Some researchers have looked into this claim and have found little corroborating evidence. Dutch political scientist Matthijs Rooduijn, from the University of Amsterdam, recently summarized the finding of his research on the political science blog *Stuk Rood Vlees*, a Dutch version of *The Monkey Cage*.[1] Based on his PhD research as well as an article with colleagues Sarah de Lange and Wouter van der Brug,[2] he concludes that mainstream parties in Western Europe have not imitated (right-wing) populist parties in terms of their populism. Similar conclusions were reached by scholars in the Baltic countries with regard to parties in Estonia, Latvia, and Lithuania. They find no strong presence of populism in terms of 'identity formation' or 'policy' among mainstream parties.[3]

This research is almost exclusively based on analyses of policy positions in party platforms. Rooduijn and colleagues looked for support for plebiscitarian politics, such as people's initiatives and referendums, which are often supported by populists, who want to 'give power back to the people' by circumventing 'the elite' of the mainstream parties. In addition, as they focused specifically on populist radical right parties, they examined the effects on immigration and integration policies. They did find clear 'imitation' effects here (see also Chapter 2).

Whether we like it or not, there is a lot of popular support for the policy positions of populist (radical right) parties in (Western) Europe. As I have shown in previous research, populist radical right parties are not a 'normal pathology' of western democracies, whose ideas are unconnected to those of the political mainstream, as is generally assumed (see Chapter 1). Rather, they are a 'pathological normalcy,' whose ideas constitute a radicalization of mainstream ideas. Consequently, large pluralities, sometimes even majorities, of the European populations support more moderate versions of their policy positions on immigration, European integration, crime, and corruption. In other words, populist radical right *light* policies, i.e. the watered-down 'imitations' proposed by mainstream parties, would be met with broad support among the population.

What is much more problematic for European democracies, particularly in the long run, is the imitation of populist discourse, particularly when *not* combined with an implementation of populist policies. And this is exactly what we are experiencing in Europe today. While mainstream political parties may not imitate populist parties in their policies, mainstream politicians do imitate populist politicians in their rhetoric, and not only during election campaigns. For example, both German Chancellor Angela Merkel and British Prime Minister David Cameron have declared that 'multi-culturalism has failed.' Similarly, virtually all mainstream politicians now proclaim to follow 'the wisdom of the people' and do their utmost to distance themselves from 'the elite.' The Dutch Balkenende IV government (2007–2010) even started its term with a 100-day bus tour through the country to ask 'the people' what they wanted.

But while the rhetoric of mainstream parties has become much more populist – a phenomenon that I have referred to as a 'populist Zeitgeist'[4] – their policies and politics have remained much the same. Neither Cameron nor Merkel has fundamentally changed their national integration policy, while Balkenende IV, and all other governments that claimed to 'listen to the people' and implement 'common sense,' largely continued the age-old policies of previous unpopular governments. Similarly, while the European elite claimed to have gotten 'the message' of the so-called 'earthquake' 2014 European elections, politics within the European Union has been business as usual (see Chapter 5).

While this might be good news for Juncker and other European elites, the exclusion of populists does not mean that Europe will remain 'governable.' In the short term, we already see more and more countries forced to change their politics-as-usual. For example, in both Greece and Sweden the rise of populist parties has forced old enemies of the centre-left and centre-right to collaborate in so-called Grand Coalitions. To be sure, Grand Coalitions are perfectly democratic, and have been common in many European democracies, such as Austria and the Netherlands, but they can further strengthen the appeal of populist parties by leaving them as the only real opposition.

Most problematic, from a long-term democratic perspective, is the growing gap between mainstream political discourse and mainstream political policies. First of all, the populist rhetoric raises the populist expectations of the population. Second, these expectations are met neither by the mainstream parties, which do not fundamentally change their policies, nor by the populist parties, which are either excluded or barely successful in implementing their policies (see Chapter 2). The consequence is a more and more dissatisfied electorate, particularly among younger groups. As the almost Europe-wide drop in election turnout shows, these dissatisfied citizens increasingly disconnect from participating in the democratic system – note that since 1999 the biggest 'party' in the European elections has been that of the non-voters (see also Chapter 15). Although Juncker might not agree, the exclusion of a majority of the population is a much bigger threat to the democratic governance of Europe than the inclusion of populist parties.

Notes

1 Matthijs Rooduijn, 'Heeft Juncker gelijk? Imiteren gevestigde partijen populisten?', *Stuk Rood Vlees*, 27 December 2014, available at http://stuk roodvlees.nl/populisme/heeft-juncker-gelijk-imiteren-gevestigde-partijen-popu listen/ (last visited 23 October 2015).
2 See Matthijs Rooduijn, *A Populist Zeitgeist? The Impact of Populism on Parties, Media and the Public in Western Europe*. Amsterdam, The Netherlands: University of Amsterdam, 2013; Matthijs Rooduijn, Sarah de Lange and Wouter van der Brug, 'A Populist Zeitgeist? Programmatic Contagion by Populist Parties in Western Europe', *Party Politics*, Vol. 20, No. 4, 2014, pp. 563–75.
3 Tallinn University Institute of Political Science and Governance/Open Estonia Foundation, *Populism in the Baltic States: A Research Report*. Tallinn, Estonia: Tallinn University Institute of Political Science and Governance/Open Estonia Foundation, 2012, available at: http://oef.org.ee/fileadmin/media/valjaanded/ uuringud/Populism_research_report.pdf (last visited 23 October 2015).
4 Cas Mudde, 'The Populist Zeitgesit', *Government and Opposition*, Vol. 39, No. 3, 2004, pp. 541–563.

9   Populism
The good, the bad and the ugly

The recent electoral success of left-wing populist parties like Syriza in Greece and Podemos in Spain has given a new impulse to the debate on populism in Europe. Until now populism was almost exclusively linked to the radical right, which led to the incorrect and unfortunate conflation of populism and xenophobia. Theoretically, populism is an ideology that considers society to be ultimately separated into two homogenous and antagonistic groups, 'the pure people' and 'the corrupt elite,' and which argues that politics should be an expression of the *volonté générale* (general will) of the people. Practically, populist actors almost always combine populism with other ideologies, such as nationalism on the right and socialism on the left.

Up until a couple of years ago the consensus position among European elites of left and right was that populism was inherently bad. It was dismissed as a 'pathology of democracy' or, as the great American historian Richard Hofstadter wrote in the 1960s, 'the paranoid style of politics.' The rise of left-wing populist movements and parties has led to a shift in the public debate, particularly pushed by followers of the late Ernesto Laclau and Chantal Mouffe, who argue that populism actually constitutes the essence of democratic politics. In their view populism is good for democracy, while liberalism is the real problem. Simply stated, both are right and wrong. The relationship between populism and liberal democracy is complex and includes the good, the bad and the ugly.

The main good is that populism mobilizes on the basis of political issues that large parts of the population care about, but that the political elites want to keep off the political agenda. Think about immigration for the populist right or austerity for the populist left. Leaders from different political parties can come together to keep issues that divide their respective electorates from the political agenda – such as European integration and immigration. In other cases they take it even a step further by excluding controversial issues from the democratic process altogether, by putting independent, technocratic institutions in charge (such as the courts or central banks). In many cases political elites worked hand in glove with cultural and economic elites, which left virtually no space for democratic opposition. Paraphrasing the Mexican political theorist Benjamin Arditi, in those cases populism behaves like the drunken guest at a dinner party, who doesn't respect the rules of public contestation and spells out painful but real problems of society.

The main bad is that populism is a monist and moralist ideology, which denies the existence of divisions of interests and opinions within 'the people' and rejects the legitimacy of political opponents. As the populists are 'the voice of the people' (*vox populi*), i.e. of *all* people, anyone with a different voice speaks for 'special interests,' i.e. the elite. Given that the key distinction is between the *pure* people and the *corrupt* elite, any compromise would lead to the *corruption* of the people and is therefore rejected. This uncompromising stand leads to a polarized political culture, in which *non*-populists turn into *anti*-populists.

Populism tends to get ugly when it gets into power. If they have to share power with non-populists the effects, positive or negative, tend to be small – think about the Austrian governments of Wolfgang Schüssel that included the populist radical right Austrian Freedom Party (FPÖ) and Alliance for the Future of Austria (BZÖ) in the 2000s. Even when populists dominate the government, as is now the case in Greece, the negative aspects of populism are often limited, although not for a lack of trying. Populists like Silvio Berlusconi in Italy, the Kaczyński brothers in Poland, or Vladimír Mečiar in Slovakia regularly tried to circumvent or undermine the power of countervailing forces, including independent judges and the political opposition. In most cases they were successfully opposed by other parts of the political structure – often with help from foreign actors, most notably the European Union.

However, the current situation in Hungary and Venezuela shows us what populism can do when it takes full control of a country. Supported by impressive popular majorities in elections, populist leaders like Viktor Orbán and Hugo Chávez have introduced new constitutions that significantly undermine the checks and balances of liberal democracy (see also Chapter 7). In addition, loyalists have been put at the head of powerful non-majoritarian institutions, such as courts and other oversight committees, often for periods that extend well beyond the legislative term. Any opposition is frustrated by a combination of legal and extra-legal pressures, from raids by tax agencies to the rejection of renewals of media licenses.

In short, populism is an illiberal democratic response to undemocratic liberalism. It criticizes the exclusion of important political issues from the political agenda by the elites and calls for their repoliticization. However, this repoliticization comes at a price. Populism's monistic views and uncompromising stand leads to a polarized society – of which, of course, both sides share responsibility – and its majoritarian extremism denies legitimacy to opponent's views and weakens the rights of minorities. While left-wing populism is often less exclusionary than right-wing populism, the main difference between them is not *whether* they exclude, but *whom* they exclude, which is largely determined by their accompanying ideology (e.g. nationalism or socialism).

10 Populism and liberal democracy

Is Greece the exception or the future of Europe?

Interview with Antonis Galanopoulos[1]

Antonis Galanopoulos (AG): What is populism? What exactly is your approach to populism?

Cas Mudde (CM): My approach is that I see populism as an ideology. By saying that populism is an ideology rather than a discourse, I assume that they mean what they say. Strictly speaking, populism is an ideology that sees society as divided into two groups; the pure people on the one hand and the corrupt elite on the other. These two groups are both homogenous and they are in an antagonistic relationship with each other.

Populists want politics to be in line with what they consider as the general will of the people. It goes back to the homogenous interpretation of the people. In my interpretation, populist actors almost always combine populism with what I call a 'host' ideology. On the right this is often an interpretation of nationalism. The host ideology, to a large extent, determines who is part of the elite and who is a part of the people. Populism, as an aspect, adds that the distinction is moral.

AG: You wrote in the Guardian (see Chapter 9) that Syriza and Podemos are characterised by an illiberalism, which is the dark side of these two parties? What elements of these parties have led you to this conclusion?

CM: What I said is that populism, in the European context, is an illiberal democratic response to undemocratic liberalism. I think that it is more in the rhetoric, the discourse, in the way the other camp is interpreted in moralistic terms and in the approach to consensus. They haven't done much yet. To me it is the interpretation of the people and believing that there is something that all people want. The implicit consequence of that is that if you don't want that, you are not really part of the people. Empirically, have they excluded someone? No. But give them four years and I think we will see it.

Again, it won't be the same as with the far right. Because I believe also in the European context, left-wing populism will emphasise inclusionary measures more than exclusionary, but the exclusionary aspects will be there. I think the struggle will be if the government wants to do something and the courts will not allow it. They will not accept the authority of the court.

AG: You mention the exclusionary aspects of left-wing populism. Who does the left-wing populism exclude and from what?

CM: There are different types of exclusion and inclusion. One of the most important is symbolic because most populist parties are discursive phenomena and because they never govern. This has to do with who is 'in' and who is 'out', who is part of 'the people' and who is not. Obviously, the assumption is that when populism comes to power, this inclusion and exclusion has a relevance to policies.

You see this more in Syriza than in Podemos. In Syriza you see the exclusion more internationally; in the way people in Syriza speak about the EU and Germany. It's not about opponents, people that have different views with whom you compromise. It is about enemies, it is about people who are bad and you can't compromise with them. You compromise with opponents, who have different views and you start to find middle ground. But you can't find middle ground if the division is moral. I think that it is problematic to see your fundamental struggle as one that doesn't allow compromise.

AG: Your focus on liberal democracy is not restrictive? What do you say about the position that the liberal and democratic traditions are confrontational and the articulation between them is merely contingent? Don't you idealise liberal democracy, risking the stigmatising of its critics, even some possibly productive critics?

CM: I don't have an explicitly normative position. I study the relationship of populism and liberal democracy. And if you are a liberal democrat, you can take things from that. If you have a different view on liberal democracy, you can take things from that too. I don't prescribe anything.

I do believe, however, that there is an inherent conflict *within* liberal democracy. Democracy is about popular sovereignty and majority will. Liberalism is about pluralism and the protection of minority rights. Majority will and minority rights can, and do, sometimes oppose each other. There is no overarching consensus on what is the right combination of them. It will always be contentious. We will always contest how much you can protect minorities and how much you can limit majority rule. It's good to make everything contentious: everything should be debated.

This is one thing that populism from both sides is doing. We have been taking away more and more things from the democratic arena. Populists re-politicise or politicise these things and that's good, because everything should be political.

Minority rights should not just be protected by an elite, because in this way they will not be fully protected. They will be fully protected only with the support of the majority. For that we should actually and explicitly talk. Not, for example, just say that gay rights are protected by the constitution. We must explain why this is so because if we don't, it can fall apart at any time. If we don't internalise the support for minority rights, they will never be safe.

AG: You set liberal democracy as a criterion. How valid is this criterion when it blurs substantial political differences, like that of the Left and Right or Socialism and Nationalism. Let me read you an extract from one of your own articles: 'Supported by impressive popular majorities in elections, populist leaders like Viktor Orbán and Hugo Chávez have introduced new constitutions that significantly undermine the checks and balances of liberal democracy.' How can we equate Orbán to Chávez?

CM: As with most comparisons, its value has limits. This is the fundamental criticism that people have against the totalitarianism theory that put Nazism and Communism together.

I believe that we can learn more about right-wing populism by looking also at left-wing populism and I also think that we can understand more about right-wing populism by looking at other right-wing parties. You must have multiple frames.

Orbán and Chávez are both examples of very powerful leaders, probably Orbán is even more powerful than Chávez ever was, and both are populists. My interest is mostly in how they affect liberal democratic institutions, how did they reform the state and in what way?

AG: You recently edited a volume entitled 'Youth and the Extreme Right.' This a very important topic with great interest for the Greek political context also, as we have seen that Golden Dawn has significant electoral appeal to younger people. So, what attracts them to the extreme right? Can you shed some light on this?

CM: Sadly enough, I can't really, because it is amazing how little research there is on youth and the extreme right. My key interest for this project was in how young people get socialised into far right ideologies and organisations. There is almost nothing on this. There are thousands of articles and books about far right parties: there are only a couple of articles about the socialisation process. This is amazing, because we all develop most of our long-lasting attitudes pretty much in our teens. So we have mainly stereotypical views.

Some of the studies show that the choice of whether or not you join a far right or a far left group is almost random. It depends on where your friends are. The other thing is that, on some occasions, it is a matter of what is available. In many communities there is only one youth club and it is run by the far right.

In Scandinavia, you see that some of the far right groups are like ethnic gangs. There are small groups of young white kids who protect themselves from other ethnic gangs. Pretty much like *American History X*. Ideology is less important than race, identity or survival. To me, most of the small far right groups are like gangs. They have nothing to do with far right parties. They have to do with the same things that drive people into gangs; the longing for protection, community, financial gain.

What's more interesting is how young people develop far right attitudes. And I think family plays a role, school plays a role, but we really don't know much about that.

AG: Do you think it is right to characterise clearly neo-Nazi parties like Golden Dawn as populist? You also choose the term 'populist radical right' instead of the term far right. The populist parties have as a nodal point the people, while the nationalist parties have the nation. Can we characterise both groups within the parties as populist?

CM: No, we can't. Actually, in the last couple of years, since 2012, most of my writings are on the far right. I use the term 'far right' because it includes both extreme right and radical right. The distinction is whether or not they support democracy. Golden Dawn is clearly anti-democratic. I don't consider Golden Dawn a populist party. I think Golden Dawn is the only relevant extreme right party in Europe.

AG: Some analysts stress the need for a strong social democracy, while others consider social democracy responsible for many negative political developments, such as the lack of political dialogue between real alternatives and the rise of right-wing populist parties. With which of the two opinions do you most agree? What are the reasons for the retreat of social democracy?

CM: Success. Hegemony makes people lazy and powerful enough to repress critics. Social democracy has gone down because of two things. First, society changed fundamentally, in a way that the old structure of the welfare state was no longer possible. I still believe that a welfare state is possible, but it has to be fundamentally reformed. Secondly, in most countries it became the party of the elite, the party of managers. It became a non-ideological, self-centred party.

I don't think that the current social democratic parties can rejuvenate themselves, because the vast majority of the current leadership has been socialised under the Third Way.[2] They are not fundamentally social democrats, they are, fundamentally, liberals. I believe that in many countries, existing social democratic parties are dying; the Netherlands is the best example. The reform will not come from them.

Sadly, in my opinion, the reform is pushed by what we now call radical left parties. Their agenda is roughly similar to the social democratic agenda of the 1960s and 1970s. The problem is that most of these parties do come from Marxist backgrounds and I don't believe they fundamentally want social democracy. Moreover, many voters will still be hesitant to trust them.

So, what we need are truly new, social democratic parties. Social democracy has to be reinvented, but solidarity should be a key value in it. Solidarity is a key term for social democracy. You can't have social democracy without it. State control of parts of the economy is fundamental, as is redistribution. If you don't have these things, you don't have social democracy.

What social democracy has to do most notably is to deal with multiculturalism, and they haven't. They had an opportunistic approach to it, trying to incorporate the migrant vote, but not really integrate the migrants. Nowadays, multiculturalism is a reality, not an ideology.

AG: Can we explain the rise of new left-wing parties in our times with the adoption of a populist strategy or a populist rhetoric?

CM: Yes, where we see the rise, we can. It is clear when you listen to [Podemost leader] Pablo Iglesias. He almost literally says: 'Look, I am a Marxist, but Marxism doesn't sell. So I have to address people in a different way.' Its meaning is: 'I have to use populism to become relevant.'

I think Syriza did the same. I don't know if they did it with the same level of consciousness and Machiavellianism, but they did it. The Socialist Party in the Netherlands, *Die Linke* in Germany have been populist at various previous times. Melenchon in France tried it, but they all had marginal success.

Given how big the crisis is, the weakness of the radical left is remarkable. Many of these parties are old parties. They are perceived as old parties, they function as old parties. They can't really modernise much. There is a big institutional problem on the Left.

AG: I will insist a little more on the new left-wing parties. Another explanation given for the rise of these parties is the role of the leadership. Pablo Iglesias and Alexis Tsipras play a key role in the success of their parties. Do you agree?

CM: I think that in modern politics you can't have a sustained political effect if you are leaderless. First of all, the media work exclusively through leaders. It's even hard to have a collective leadership these days, because the media want to have one face for every party. You see that even in some left-wing parties that have co-leaders. Most of the time, one of them will become the face of the party.

A leaderless movement has two problems. First of all, it doesn't have one face and second it has too many faces, and that means that everyone can interpret it. Occupy Wall Street is a very good example and the *Indignados* was a good example, but Pablo Iglesias is now hegemonic in his interpretation of the *Indignados*, because he is the face and he knows how to play the system.

I strongly believe that it wasn't Syriza, a coalition of radical left groups, which won the elections. It was what Tsipras stood for. He stands for a new generation of principled but pragmatic leaders, not that of old-school small Marxist-Leninist ideological groups. He has a popular support for that agenda, they are not supporting him as the Messiah, they are supporting him as the voice of that agenda. That's not necessarily the same agenda as the organisations under him have.

The question is: who has the power? In that sense, Iglesias is in a much better position in Podemos. He has no old structures to fight. He has redefined the Indignados, giving it probably a narrower and a more social democratic, old socialist interpretation. He is the party. But I think that the success of Syriza is not going to be copied by Podemos. I think that Greece is the exception. Greece is not the future of Europe.

Notes

1   Antonis Galanopoulos is a graduate student in Political Theory and Philosophy at Aristotle University of Thessaloniki in Greece. The interview was conducted in Thessaloniki on March 23, 2015.

2   I have discussed this in more details in 'Nothing Left? In Search of (a New) Social Democracy', *Open Democracy*, 21 November 2013, available at https://www.opendemocracy.net/can-europe-make-it/cas-mudde/nothing-left-in-search-of-new-social-democracy (last visited 9 November 2015).

11 Populism

A primer

Already in April 2010, a good five years before a populist coalition government would be formed in Greece, then EU President Herman van Rompuy called populism 'the greatest danger for Europe' in an interview with the German *Frankfurter Allgemeine Zeitung*. Since then, many establishment voices have done the same, from German Chancellor Angela Merkel to the editors of the *New York Times*. What all warnings have in common is that they (1) come from people in power; (2) are vague on the exact meaning of populism; and (3) claim that populism is (omni)present in European politics.

Historically populism has been a marginal political phenomenon in Europe, unlike in the Americas (North and South). In recent years populist parties of left and right have gained electoral successes throughout Europe, although their effects on European politics have so far remained fairly limited.

What populism is (not)

Populism as a buzzword in the media around the world. There is virtually not a politician who has not been labeled populist at one time. In fact, accused would be a better term, as most people use populism is a *Kampfbegriff* (fighting word) to defame a political opponent. Few politicians self-identify as populist. Those who do usually first redefine the term in a way that is closer to the popular use of democracy than of populism.

In the public debate populism is mostly used to denounce a form of politics that uses (a combination of) demagogy, charismatic leadership, or a *Stammtisch* (pub table) discourse. None of the three are accurate understandings of populism. While some populists might promise everything to everyone (i.e. demagogy) or speak a simple, even vulgar, language (i.e. *Stammtisch* discourse), many do not. More importantly, many non-populist populists also do this, particularly during election campaigns. Similarly, while some successful populists are charismatic leaders, some are not, and many successful non-populists are also considered charismatic.

Instead, populism is best defined as a thin-centred ideology that considers society to be ultimately separated into two homogeneous and antagonistic groups, 'the pure people' and 'the corrupt elite', and which argues that politics should be an expression of the *volonté general* (general will) of the people. This means that populism is a particular view on how society is and should be structured, but it addresses only a limited part of the larger political agenda. For example, it says little about the ideal economic or political system that a (populist) state should have. Its essential features are: morality and monism.

The key point is that populism sees both groups as essentially homogeneous, i.e. without fundamental internal divisions, and considers the essence of the division between the two groups to be moral. Consequently, its main opposites are elitism and pluralism. Elitism sees the same major division, but considers the elite to be pure and the people as corrupt. Pluralism has a fundamentally different worldview than both elitism and populism, seeing society as divided into several groups with different interests and favoring a politics based on consensus between these groups.

Contrary to what defenders and opponents may claim, populism is neither the *essence* nor the *negation* of democracy. To put it simply, populism is pro-democracy, but anti-liberal democracy. It supports popular sovereignty and majority rule, but rejects pluralism and minority rights. In the European context, populism can be seen as an illiberal democratic answer to problems created by an undemocratic liberalism. Criticizing the decade-old trend to depoliticize controversial issues by placing them outside of the national democratic (i.e. electoral) realm, by transferring them to supranational institutions like the European Union (EU) or to (neo-)liberal institutions like courts and central banks, populists call for the *re*-politicization of issues like European integration, gay rights, or immigration.

A final point to note is that populism is neither right nor left, or, perhaps better, populism can be found on both the left and the right. This is not exactly the same as saying that populism is like a 'chameleon,' as it is not necessarily the same populist actor who changes colors. Populism rarely exists in a pure form, in the sense that most populist actors combine it with another ideology. This so-called host ideology, which tends to be very stable, is either left or right. Generally, left populists will combine populism with some interpretation of socialism, while right populists will combine it with some form of nationalism. Today populism is more on the left in Southern Europe and more on the right in Northern Europe.

Populism in Europe

Although populism has a long history in Europe, it has always been a marginal political phenomenon. It emerged for the first time in Russia in the late-nineteenth century. The so-called *Narodniki* were a relatively small group of urban elites who unsuccessfully tried to stir a peasant revolt. While unsuccessful in Russia, Nardoniki did have a strong influence in Eastern Europe, where several agrarian populist parties existed in the early 20th century. Most of these groups had little political influence in the largely authoritarian states of that period. And while both communism and fascism used populist rhetoric, particularly during the movement stage, both ideologies and regimes were essentially elitist.

Post-war Europe saw very little populism until the 1990s. There was *Poujadism* in France in the late-1950s, the Danish and Norwegian Progress Parties in the 1970s, and PASOK in the 1980s, but all these movements were largely *sui genesis* rather than part of a broader populist moment. This changed with the rise of the populist radical right in the late 1980s. Although the oldest parties of this group, like the National Front (FN) in France and the Flemish Bloc (now Flemish Interest, VB) in Belgium, started out as elitist parties, they soon embraced a populist platform with slogans like 'We Say What You Think' and 'The Voice of the People.' In recent years a new left populism has also emerged in some countries, particularly in Southern Europe.

Table 11.1 lists the most important populist parties in Europe today – only the most successful party in each country is included. The third column gives the electoral result in the most recent European election of May 2014, which vary from 51.5 per cent to 3.7 per cent of the vote – note that countries without a successful populist party are excluded (e.g. Luxembourg, Portugal or Slovenia). On average, populist parties gained some 12.5 per cent of the vote in the last European elections; not insignificant, but hardly a 'political earthquake' as the international media claimed (see Chapter 5).

A better insight into the electoral and political relevance of populist parties is provided by the results in the most recent national elections. The fourth column gives the result of the most successful populist party in the country; the fifth column, its ranking among all national parties; the sixth, the total electoral support of *all* populist parties in the country; and the seventh column, the change in the total populist vote between the most recent and the previous national election. Here are the most important lessons to be drawn.

First, populist parties are electorally successful in most European countries. In roughly 20 European countries a populist party gains at least 10 per cent of the national vote. Second, all populist parties together score

Table 11.1 Main populist party results in 2014 European elections and most recent national election (and change to previous similar election)

Country	Populist party	% EP14	% Nat	Rank	% Total	% Change
Austria	Austrian Freedom Party (FPÖ)	19.7	20.5	3	29.8	+1.5
Belgium	Flemish Interest (VB)	4.1	3.7	10	5.6	−5.7
Bulgaria	Bulgaria Without Censorship (BBT)	10.7	5.7	6	10.2	+2.9
Denmark	Danish People's Party (DPP)	26.6	12.3	3	12.3	−1.5
Finland	Finns Party (PS)	12.9	19.1	2	17.7	−1.4
France	National Front (FN)	25.0	13.6	3	20.5	+16.2
Germany	The Left	7.3	8.6	3	10.5	−1.0
Greece	Coalition of the Radical Left (Syriza)	26.6	36.3	1	42.1	+6.1
Hungary	Fidesz – Hungarian Civic Alliance (Fidesz)	51.5	44.5	1	65.0	−4.3
Ireland	Sinn Fein (SF)	19.5	9.9	4	11.3	+3.7
Italy	Five Star Movement (M5S)	21.2	25.6	1	51.3	+5.6
Lithuania	Order and Justice (TT)	14.3	7.3	4	7.3	−5.4
Netherlands	Party for Freedom (PVV)	13.2	10.1	3	19.8	−5.6
Norway	Progress Party (FrP)	–	16.3	3	16.3	−6.6
Poland	Law and Justice (PiS)	31.8	29.9	2	39.9	+7.8
Romania	People's Party – Dan Diaconescu (PP-DD)	3.7	14.7	3	16.1	+13.0
Slovakia	Direction-Social Democracy (Smer-SD)	24.1	44.4	1	63.4	+11.4
Spain	We Can (Podemos)	8.0	–	–	–	–
Sweden	Sweden Democrats (SD)	9.7	12.9	3	12.9	+7.2
Switzerland	Swiss People's Party (SVP)	–	26.6	1	27.8	−1.7
UK	United Kingdom Independence Party (UKIP)	27.5	3.1	3	13.2	+7.6

an average of ca. 16.5 per cent of the vote in national elections. This ranges from a staggering 65 per cent in Hungary, shared between Fidesz and the Movement for a Better Hungary (Jobbik), to 5.6 per cent in Belgium. Third, while the overall trend is up, most populist parties are electorally volatile. Few populist parties have been able to establish themselves as relatively stable political forces in their national party system. Fourth, there are huge cross-national and cross-temporal differences within Europe. While some populist parties are brand-new (e.g. M5S and Podemos), others are several decades old (e.g. FN, FPÖ, The Left, SVP). Similarly, whereas some parties are on the up (e.g. DF, Syriza, UKIP), others are in a downfall (e.g. PP-DD and VB).

When we are focusing only on the (minority of) European countries where populism is a major political phenomenon, there are four important conclusions to draw. First, in five countries a populist party is the biggest political party – Greece, Hungary, Italy, Slovakia, and Switzerland. Second, populist parties gained a majority of votes in three countries – Hungary, Italy, and Slovakia. However, in at least two of these countries the main populist parties are strongly opposed to collaboration. The situation in Hungary is most striking, as both its main governmental party (Fidesz) and its main opposition party (Jobbik) is populist. Third, populist parties are currently in the national government in seven countries – Finland, Greece, Hungary, Lithuania, Norway, Slovakia, and Switzerland. Greece is unique in that it has a populist coalition government of a left and a right populist party. Fourth, and final, in six countries a populist party is part of the established political parties – Hungary, Italy, Lithuania, Poland, Slovakia, and Switzerland. This is important to note, as populism is normally associated exclusively with challenger parties and deemed incapable of establishing itself in a political system. Yet, while populist parties have to be extra careful not to be considered part of 'the elite,' populists like former Italian premier Silvio Berlusconi and current Hungarian premier Viktor Orbán have been successful at retaining their cleverly constructed 'outsider' status in power.

Why is populism successful (now)?

Given the immense academic interest in the phenomenon of populism one would assume that we have a good understanding of why populist parties are successful and, even more specifically, under which circumstances they rise and decline. This is not the case. Most analyses of European populism focus almost exclusively on one type of populist parties, notably the populist radical right, and particularly its non-populist aspects. However, immigration has little explanatory power for populist parties in countries that have little immigration (like Hungary and Poland) or for populist parties that don't oppose immigration (such as Podemos or Syriza). At the same time, the most popular theories are often too broad and vague (see Chapter 1).

While crisis and globalization have some relationship to the rise of populism, globalization is related to everything and crisis is usually undefined and simply used whenever a populist party becomes successful (making the 'theory' tautological). The following six reasons are also still too broad and vague, but indicate some important factors that address both the demand-side and supply-side of populist politics.

First, large parts of the European electorates believe that important issues are not (adequately) addressed by the political elites. This relates to issues like European integration and immigration, on which established parties have long been unwilling to campaign, as well as socio-economic issues like unemployment and welfare state reform, particularly in light of the current economic crisis. While it seems fair to argue that political elites have indeed been less forthcoming and successful in addressing important issues, and to a larger extent than in previous periods (i.e. before the 1990s), what is more important to note is that large parts of the European populations have come to *perceive* this as a major problem. This has created widespread political dissatisfaction, which is a fertile breeding ground for populist parties, but also for other anti-establishment parties, such as Citizens (*Ciudadanos*) in Spain.

Second, national political elites are increasingly perceived as being 'all the same.' Again, the perception is more important than the reality, although the two are not unrelated. While commentators have decried the so-called 'end of ideology' since the late 1960s, there is little doubt that the situation today is much more extreme. Responding to the structural transformation of European societies as a consequence of the 'post-industrial revolution,' including the decline of the working class and secularization, the main established parties have moderated their ideologies and converged strongly on both socio-cultural and socio-economic issues. The emergence of the '*neue Mitte*' (new centre) and 'Third Way' on the centre-left, which by and large transformed social democratic parties into centre-right parties targeting the same voters as the Christian democratic and conservative-liberal parties, alienated a large part of the remaining ('native') working class and left more ideological voters of both left and right without a political voice.

Third, more and more people see the national political elites as essentially powerless. Again, perception and reality are closely linked, even if many people will not necessarily be accurately informed. In the past decades European elites have engaged in one of the most amazing transfers of power from the national to the supranational level. Rarely have politicians so happily marginalized themselves. Of particular importance was the Maastricht Treaty of 1992, which has taken many important issues out of the national democratic realm and transferred them to the much less democratic and transparent EU sphere. This was, of course, most notably the case for the countries that joined the Eurozone, which no longer control their own currency or monetary policy.

Fourth, at the same time, the process of 'cognitive mobilization' has made the European people better educated and more independent, and consequently more critical and less deferential toward the political elites. Getting mixed messages from the political elites, who claim to be powerless in the case of unpopular policies ('the results of the EU/globalization/US') but in full control in the case of popular policies ('my successful economic policies'), European populations feel confident to judge their politicians to be incompetent or even deceitful.

Fifth, the media structure has become much more favorable to political challengers. Until at least the 1980s the established parties controlled most of the important media in Europe, be it party-owned newspapers or state-owned radio and television controlled by parties-appointed boards. While active censorship was rare, most journalists self-censored stories that challenged the interests and values of the political mainstream. Consequently, critique of immigration or European integration was long marginalized, while major corruption, particularly involving elites from several established parties, was left uncovered. This is no longer possible in a world dominated by party-independent, private media and an uncontrollable Internet. Not only do all stories and voices find an outlet, populist stories and voices are particularly attractive to a media dominated by an economic logic. After all, scandals and controversy sell!

Finally, while the previous five factors have created a fertile breeding ground and favourable 'discursive opportunity structure' for populists, the success of populist parties like the FN or Syriza is also related to the fact that populist actors have become much more attractive to voters (and the media). Almost all successful populist parties have skillful people at the top, including media-savvy leaders like Beppe Grillo (M5S), Pablo Iglesias (Podemos) or Geert Wilders (PVV). They can not only hold their own in political debates with leaders of established parties, but they are often much more adept at exploiting the huge potential of new resources, such as social media. For example, for years Wilders dominated the Dutch political debate purely through Twitter. Just one well-constructed tweet would be picked up by journalists, who would then force established politicians to respond, and thereby helped Wilders set the political agenda and frame the political debate.

Part III
Euroscepticism

12 European integration
After the fall

For decades the process of European integration was an elite-driven process supported by a 'permissive consensus' of the masses. While the masses were hardly involved in shaping the process of integration, and were almost never asked for their explicit approval (in elections or referendums), the elites could count on a basic level of unexpressed support. With the rise of so-called 'Euroscepticism,' at least since the signing of the Maastricht Treaty in 1992, which transformed the mainly economic European Community into a much more political and social European Union (EU), this permissive consensus is no longer a given. In fact, with popular revolts like the rejection of the European Convention in referendums in France and the Netherlands in 2005, some commentators have started to speak of a 'constraining dissensus.'

Recent events have shown that this dissensus exists not only at the mass level. While Euroscepticism has for long been limited to minor parties on the political fringes, notably on the radical left and right, it has well established itself in today's political mainstream. For instance, the (soft) Eurosceptic European Conservatives and Reformists (ECR) is the fourth largest political group in the current European Parliament, and it includes, among others, the main right-wing parties in the Czech Republic, Poland, and the United Kingdom (see Chapter 16).

The current economic crisis has undermined the permissive consensus even further. For the first time many Europeans are directly faced with consequences of European integration. The idea that Bulgarians and Slovaks have to bail out Greeks and Portuguese to ensure that their social benefits are at times better than their own, has had a profound effect on people's perceptions of the EU. No longer is European integration simply a good, if abstract, idea, with some tangible positive effects (e.g. the Euro, no border controls); from now on, Europeans are truly aware of (some of) the economic and financial consequences of European integration, and many people, particularly in the Northwest, are not amused.

In addition to the changing perceptions of the European masses, the European elites have changed their opinions too. Although the exact start of the 'crisis of the European idea' is difficult to pinpoint, the last decades have shown little elite debate about Europe's future. With the exception of people like Belgian ex-premier Guy Verhofstadt, now chairperson of the Alliance of Liberals and Democrats for Europe (ALDE) group in the European Parliament, no important politicians openly defend a federalist Europe anymore. In fact, whether Europhile or Europhobic, no major politician or party group propagates a clear and elaborate ideal of European integration!

The void of debates on the future is filled by the actual and symbolic consequences of recent actions and debates. Let me just focus on two of the most important. The first action is the recent decision of the Danish government to re-impose border controls, in an alleged effort to stem the entrance of East European criminals. While the border controls will be enforced by custom agents, rather than by border guards, this still directly opposes the spirit, if not the law, of the Schengen Treaty, which regulates the free transfer of people within the EU.

The second is the debate about the Euro and the Eurozone, which predates the recent economic crisis but is heightened by it. In the past couple of years high-ranking politicians in countries like Greece and Italy have speculated about a possible withdrawal from the Eurozone. While no concrete action has been taken, so far, and most of the politicians have denied their intention when confronted with media and political pressure, the current debate about the Eurozone is no longer only about who is going to join next, but also about who might be better (off) leaving it.

The major significance of both developments is at this time not so much practical but psychological. For the first time since the start of the process of European integration, now more than fifty years ago, the implicit idea of uninterrupted progress toward further integration is challenged both in ideas and practices and by both elites and masses. More than ever before there is a need for an open debate on European integration, but this time a debate that explores all options, including the return to a *less* integrated EU. This requires courage and vision from all political actors, Europhile and Europhobic alike, as the economical, political and social consequences of European integration are too far-reaching to have the process linger on without any clear direction.

13 The European elites' politics of fear

Fear mongering by political elites is nothing new. In fact, influential political thinkers from the Italian Renaissance philosopher Niccolo Machiavelli (1469–1527) to the German constitutional jurist Carl Schmitt (1888–1985) have argued that creating antagonisms and fear constitute the essence of politics. Thousands of articles have been devoted to the 'politics of fear' towards 'others' in recent decades. Particularly in the European context, they have pointed out how European elites have created stereotypical images of (mostly Muslim) immigrants – as homogeneous, fundamentalist, anti-western or pre-modern, authoritarian, violent, etc. – and exaggerated claims of an apocalyptic future – in which minarets have replaced church towers, Muslim majorities oppress 'native' minorities, etc.

But another type of fear mongering by European elites has met almost no criticism and has remained unstudied, so far. I refer here to the EU elite's long-standing warning against alleged threats from so-called 'anti-Europeans,' by which they mostly mean Eurosceptics (see also Chapter 5). At stake here is not just the (imagined) national communities or states of Europe, but the (imagined) European community and state, as embodied by the EU. This politics of fear follows the same mechanism as those described above: opponents are essentialized and homogenized, while an apocalyptic future is presented, which, of course, can only be prevented if the policies of the elite are followed. Eurosceptics are 'anti-European populists' that are 'nationalist' or even 'anti-democratic,' while the future is one of political crisis or, worse, war. The most alarming statement in this long tradition came last week from the prime minister of Luxemburg, Jean-Claude Juncker. In an interview with the German magazine *Der Spiegel*, on 11 March 2013, the retired head of the Eurogroup (and now EU President) said: 'I am chilled by the realization of how similar circumstances in Europe in 2013 are to those of 100 years ago' (see also Chapter 8).

What did Juncker mean? What is the EU elite warning us against/of? Whether referring back to 1913 or 1933, the message is the same: Europe is again at the brink of a massive political crisis at best, and a European war at worst! In June 2010 EU Commission President José Manuel Barroso warned that democracy could 'collapse' in Southern Europe, while EU President Herman van Rompuy has regularly warned against the 'winds of populism,' which he considers the biggest threat to Europe.

The economic crisis has heightened the discourse of the threat of another European war. In the past years various high-ranking European politicians have warned of the threat of war should the euro collapse – including British Business Secretary Vince Cable, German Chancellor Angela Merkel, and Polish Finance Minister Jacek Rostowski. While these warnings have been headed more frequently in recent years, they are not new to the crisis era. For example, in the Dutch campaign in the run-up to the European referendum in 2005, Economics Minister Laurens Jan Brinkhorst warned that, were the Dutch people to reject the Treaty Establishing A Constitution for Europe, generally (if wrongly) referred to as the European Constitution, 'the light would go off' in the Netherlands.

From an economical point of view, the analogy of 1933 and 2013 makes some sense. While the structure of national and global economics has changed fundamentally in the past century, in both periods a banking crisis caused a global economic crisis, which hit (parts of) Europe particularly hard. However, from a political point of view the similarities are much less clear.

While it is true that 'Not since World War II have extreme and populist forces had so much influence on the national parliaments as they have today,' as EU Home Affairs Commissioner Cecilia Malmström recently declared, this is only part of the story. First, 'extreme and populist forces' are represented in the national parliaments of only about one half of the EU member states, depending slightly on the interpretation of the terms. Second, while they do have more influence than ever before in the postwar era, they still constitute (small) parliamentary minorities in most countries, with virtually no representation in national governments (see Chapters 2 and 3).

Even more importantly, while (liberal) democracy lacked majority support among large parts (often majorities) of the European elites and masses in the first decades of the 20th century, today the democratic ideal is truly hegemonic. In fact, whereas in 1933 many of the few democratic countries were governed by reluctant democrats and challenged by fundamental anti-democrats, today both the establishment and its main challengers are fundamentally democratic, and the latter at best reluctantly liberal. Moreover, as a consequence of the, admittedly unequal, development of welfare states across the continent, the economic hardship experienced as a consequence of the current crisis, while brutal and inhumane in many cases, is softened by welfare measures that have prevented life-threatening poverty for most European citizens.

But what about Greece? Here the 'anti-European populists' (Monti) gained almost half of the votes in the (first) 2012 elections, unemployment is at – or even above – early-20th century levels, poverty is truly threatening the lives of hundreds of thousands of Greeks, and political violence of left and right seems an almost daily occurrence. Moreover, Greece is indeed the one country where 'neo-nazis have been elected' (Malmström) to parliament – one could perhaps also include Jobbik in Hungary.

Although I do consider mass support of extremist parties like Golden Dawn (XA) and, to a certain extent, the Communist Party of Greece (KKE) as warning signs of truly anti-democratic sentiments within a society, there are some important side notes to be made (see also Chapters 10 and 19). First, together these two extremist parties attracted around ten per cent of the Greek people in the June 2012 election! Even in the most favourable polls, the vast majority of Greeks continue to support democratic parties; even if they might be Eurosceptic. Second, Greece is not Europe. Not now and not in the (near) future! In fact, Greece has always been an outlier, even within Southern Europe, in terms of both the strength of 'extreme and populist forces' and the failures of the liberal democratic state. Not surprising, then, that the mass political protests in Portugal and Spain have been organized predominantly by clearly pro-liberal democratic, and often pro-European (i.e. EU), groups, and 'extreme and populist forces' have played little role in elections.

Many fear mongers identify Germany as the main cause of the lack of European solidarity and, thus (in their mind), the threat of a new European war. Almost excusing the fierce, and sometimes violent, anti-German sentiments in Southern Europe, Juncker said: 'The way some German politicians have lashed out at Greece when the country fell into the crisis has left deep wounds there.' Similarly, academics like the British historian Niall Ferguson and the American economist Nouriel Roubini, eagerly given voice by pro-EU media, warned that Germany 'would do well to remember how a European banking crisis two years before 1933 contributed directly to the breakdown of democracy not just in their own country but right across the European continent.'

Let's see how Germany has behaved within the European context over the past five years. Germany has approved every single bailout of a EU member state with large parliamentary majorities, and has already invested close to 500 billion euro in the various bailout and stability measures. Not exactly a new German *Sonderweg* (special path). And the so maligned German Chancellor Angela Merkel has declared her unwavering support for the process of European integration, including a further deepening of the EU, throughout the crisis. In fact, she has at times sounded as one of the EU fear mongers: 'Nobody should take for granted another 50 years of peace and prosperity in Europe. They are not for granted. That's why I say: if the euro fails, Europe fails.' Hardly a modern-day Adolf Hitler!

In short, there is not much evidence that European democracy, at the national or EU level, is being threatened by either the national elites or the masses. While protest parties are registering record scores in several national elections (see Chapter 11), many of these parties, even the so-called populist ones, are reformist rather than revolutionary, with regard to both national democracy and European integration. In fact, the real threat for the EU fear mongers does not come from true anti-democrats or anti-Europeans (in the restricted sense of anti-EU), but from democratic Eurosceptics, who want to fundamentally transform, rather than abolish, the EU. Juncker admitted as much when he said: 'Of course politicians should respect the will of the people as much as possible, provided they adhere to the European treaties.' Asked whether this also applies to policies opposed by a majority of the people, he clarified: 'This means, if need be, that they have to pursue the right policies, even if many voters think they are the wrong ones.'

It is exactly this form of 'enlightened Europeanism' that constitutes the true danger to both national democracy and European integration today. By forcing national governments to continue on a path of European integration that is not, or no longer, supported by the majority of their population, they breed and radicalize anti-democratic and anti-EU sentiments. Fully aware of this, the EU elite increasingly constrain the already limited avenues for democratic popular control of the process of European integration, most notably by pressuring national governments to refrain from referendums on important EU decisions – as was the case in Greece, Ireland, the Netherlands, etc. Importantly, this does not only harm the democratic basis of the EU, which was never particularly strong anyway, but slowly erodes the democratic basis of its member states too. Now *that* is something to be fearful of!

14 What will the European elections bring the Western Balkans?

The upcoming European elections of 22–25 May 2014 have generated unprecedented media attention inside and outside of the European Union (EU). Despite the fact that the lack of serious election campaigns in most EU countries confirms the enduring 'second-order' status of the European elections, i.e. secondary in importance to national parliamentary elections (see Chapter 5), the national and international media attention reflects the EU's increased role in the lives of people inside and outside of its territory. This relevance is probably nowhere as big as in Southeastern Europe, where most countries are in the waiting room of the EU. What will the European elections bring them?

At first sight it looks like the European elections are not going to bring them anything good. If one is to believe the international media, as well as prominent commentators and European politicians, the elections will bring a victory of 'anti-European populists' and will create a 'self-hating European Parliament.' Far right parties in particular are expected to win big. While they might disagree on their exact position towards the EU – some Euro-sceptic parties demand fundamental reform (e.g. the Austrian Freedom Party and Belgian Flemish Interest), while others want their country to 'exit' the EU (e.g. the Dutch Party for Freedom and the French National Front) – all anti-European parties agree that there should be less EU in terms of both deepening and widening (see Chapter 6).

While the most ferocious opposition to further enlargement is usually reserved for Turkey, which the far right consider a 'Muslim Trojan Horse,' Southeast European countries should not expect much more sympathy. Although some far right parties used to hold relatively close ties to similar parties in former Yugoslavia in the 1990s, notably the French National Front and the Serbian Radical Party, new party leaderships and sharpened anti-European positions have made these ties obsolete or irrelevant. For most anti-European populists the countries of the Western Balkans are not ready for EU membership at best, and 'corrupt robbers' nests' that should never be admitted at worst. In addition, the sizeable Muslims populations in Albania, Bosnia-Herzegovina and Kosovo are easy targets for Islamophobic campaigns that fuel anti-enlargement positions.

This all notwithstanding, anti-EUropean parties are not going to rule the EU anytime soon. Even in the wildest prognostics, which are based on pure sensationalist speculation, anti-EUropean parties will get a maximum of one-third of the seats in the next European Parliament (EP) – and this includes far left as well as 'soft' right-wing Eurosceptic parties, which are much less adamantly opposed to EU enlargement into the Western Balkans (see Chapter 16). Given that EP decisions require a regular majority, which the established pro-European centre-right EEP-ED and centre-left S&D political groups will easily get, even without the usual support of the liberal ALDE, one-third of the seats will give them little political power (see Chapter 6).

On top of that, the EP is only one of the three main political institutions in the EU, and the only one that anti-EUropean populists will have representation in. Just two EU governments have some far right presence – the National Alliance is a junior partner in the Latvian coalition government and Attack supports the Bulgarian minority government – and even in these cases they will not have a representative in the European Commission or in the European Council of Heads of State or Government. In other words, although anti-EUropean parties will probably gain their best results in the upcoming European elections, they will remain irrelevant political actors within the EU.

This is not to say that their expected electoral success will have no influence on the politics of the EU and its member states. As long as anti-EUropean populists will win at least some seats, most of the international media will focus a disproportionate part of their coverage of the European elections on them. The message will be that 'Europeans turned their back on Europe' and mainstream parties will feel the need to respond to stave off electoral defeats in the (more important) national parliamentary elections in the future – such as in Sweden (September 2014) and, in particular, the United Kingdom (2015). While the main response will be in terms of rhetoric rather than policy, this will certainly not speed up the accession process of the Southeast European countries. At the same time, it will also not fundamentally change their accession status.

But although the European elections will not fundamentally change the relationships between the EU and the countries of the Western Balkans, it is important to note that 'Europe' *has* changed substantially. The economic crisis and the EU responses to it, most notably the controversial combination of austerity and bailouts, has not only deeply affected Europe's economies but also its populations. Support for the EU has tanked, with a plurality –

and no longer a majority – of European holding a positive view of the EU. Euroscepticism has reached an all-time high with remarkably large minorities of Europeans losing faith in the project altogether and supporting an exit of their country from the EU. And while I haven't seen any reliable surveys on attitudes towards further enlargement, it seems safe to assume that enlargement fatigue is much more widespread among Europe's masses than among the EU's elites.

In summary, even though the European elections will not fundamentally change EU policies, and Southeast European countries can still expect to join the EU at some point in the future, they will have to realize that they are going to become part of a very different EU than they applied to years ago. Today the EU is economically and politically weakened and run by a shrinking pro-European elite who lacks a clear ideological vision of, and a popular mandate for, either deepening or widening the EU.

15 The 2014 European elections in numbers

The 2014 European elections have led to a surprising amount of media attention and speculation. The dominant frame, which had been decided upon well before the actual results came in, is that 'the far right' or 'Euro-scepticism' has won the elections. In fact, we are told that there has been an 'earthquake' that has lead to 'concerns in Europe' (see also Chapter 5). The new European Parliament (EP) will 'struggle to find majorities,' divided as it is between a pro-EU and an anti-EU camp.

But behind this simplistic and sensationalist narrative lays a deeply fragmented reality of an EP with over 100 national parties. In many ways, this reflects an ongoing trend of fractionalization in national party systems, in which big parties are shrinking, or even disappearing, the number of represented parties is growing, and turnout is (on average) dwindling.

I'll present some of these trends in a set of remarkable numbers from the 2014 European elections (see Table 14.1).[1] I have not systematically compared them to similar numbers in the 2009 European elections or the last national parliamentary elections. My hunch is that the 2014 European elections continued a broader trend, but with important national and, to some extent, regional differences. The biggest shocks were in Southern Europe and Western Europe, while Eastern Europe was remarkably stable on average.[2]

Medium (M) is the new Large (L)

Scholars started to note the decline of the Grand Old European parties in the 1980s, but it has become particularly visible in the 21st century. Given that one of the golden rules of second-order elections is that 'big parties lose,' we wouldn't expect too many big parties in the 2014 European elections. And this was exactly what happened, but to an even larger extent than previously.

53.4: The highest percentage of votes for one single party in the 2014 European elections. With it, the Maltese Labour Party (PL/MLP) was only

Table 15.1 The 2014 European elections in numbers: parties and turnout[3]

Country	% Vote Biggest Party	# Parties > 33%	# Parties > 25%	% Turnout	% Two Biggest Parties	# Parties for >50%	# Parties with MEPs
Austria	27.0	0	2	45.7	51.1	2	5
Belgium	16.4	0	0	90.0	28.9	4	10
Bulgaria	30.5	0	1	35.5	49.6	3	5
Croatia	41.4*	1*	2*	25.1	81.3*	2*	5*
Cyprus	37.7	1	2	44.0	64.6	2	4
Czech Rep	16.1	0	0	19.5	32.1	4	7
Denmark	26.6	0	1	56.4	45.7	3	7
Estonia	24.3	0	0	36.4	46.7	3	5
Finland	22.6	0	0	40.9	42.3	3	7
France	25.0	0	1	43.5	45.8	3	7
Germany	35.3	1	2	47.9	62.6	2	13
Greece	26.6	0	1	58.2	49.3	3	6
Hungary	51.5	1	1	28.9	66.2	1	6
Ireland	24.0	0	0	51.6	46.0	3	3
Italy	40.8	1	1	60.0	62.0	2	7
Latvia	46.0	1	1	30.4	60.0	2	6
Lithuania	17.4	0	0	44.9	34.7	3	7
Luxembourg	37.7	1	1	90.0	52.7	2	4
Malta	53.4	2	2	74.8	93.4	1	2
Netherlands	15.4	0	0	37.0	30.4	4	10
Poland	32.3	0	2	22.7	63.6	2	5
Portugal	31.5	0	2*	34.5	59.2*	2*	5*
Romania	37.6*	1	1	32.2	52.6	2	6
Slovakia	24.1	0	0	13.0	37.3	4	8
Slovenia	24.9	0	0	21.0	40.5	3*	5*
Spain	26.1	0	1	45.9	46.1	3	12
Sweden	24.4	0	0	48.8	39.7	3	9
UK	26.8	0	1	36.0	51.5	2	10
EU	30.1	10	25	43.1	51.3	2.5	6.7

* At least one of the parties involved is an electoral coalition.

one of two parties to get a majority of the vote; the other was Fidesz with
51.5 per cent in Hungary. Perhaps even more striking, in just three other
countries did the biggest party get more than 40 per cent: Croatian
Democratic Union (HDZ) with 41.4 per cent in Croatia, the Democratic Party
(PD) with 40.8 per cent in Italy, and Unity (V) with 46.0 per cent in Latvia.
In all these cases the parties were either current (HDZ+) or former electoral
alliances that had since merged into one political party (PD and V).

15.4: The lowest per centage of a biggest party in a country. Surprisingly, it was in the Netherlands and not Belgium, despite the fact that in the latter country no political party contests elections throughout the whole territory! In a total of four countries the biggest party attracted less than 20 per cent of the vote (Belgium, Czech Republic, Lithuania, and Netherlands).

1: Only one country had two parties with more than 33 per cent of the vote each – Malta – the last remaining true two-party system in the EU. In a staggering two-thirds of the 28 EU member states not one party was able to win at least one-third of the vote, while in a quarter of the countries the biggest party attracted less than one-quarter of the votes.

A fragmented European Parliament

411: The number of seats that the two largest political groups in the European Parliament, the European People's Party (EPP) and the Progressive Alliance of Socialists and Democrats (S&D), hold together. Through a decrease of 59 MEPs, though in a slightly smaller parliament, it gives the two strongly pro-EU groups a majority of 54.7 per cent of the seats – 6.7 per cent less than in the previous parliament. However, it can count on the support of the Alliance of Liberals and Democrats in Europe (ALDE), which has been reduced to 59 seats (from 83), in virtually all important decisions.

186: The total number of political parties that have representatives in the 2014–19 European Parliament. This is an increase of 16 parties compared to the 2009 elections, despite the fact that the EP decreased its total number of seats from 766 to 751. It should be noted that several of these parties are in fact electoral coalitions, so the actual number of parties with MEPs will probably be around 200.

43: The largest number of seats for one individual party, although technically the Christian Democratic Union (CDU) is a coalition of CDU and Christian Social Union (CSU), its more conservative Bavarian counterpart. It is thereby 12 seats bigger than the second-biggest faction, that of the Italian Democratic Party (PD), but eight seats smaller than it was in the last legislature – again, it should be noted that the 2014–19 EP is 15 seats smaller than its predecessor.

37: The number of new parties in the 2014–19 EP. Although twenty member states saw a new party enter the EP, Germany alone accounted for eight (21.6 per cent), a consequence of the Constitutional Court's decision to strike down the electoral threshold of 3 per cent. By far the biggest new party is Italy's Five Star Movement (M5S), which gained 17 seats.

21: The number of parties that lost representation in the EP. Interestingly, given the narrative of the 'earthquake of far right success' (see Chapter 5), is that no less than five far right parties lost representation: Ataka (Bulgaria), British National Party (UK), Popular Orthodox Rally (Greece), Greater Romania Party (Romania), and the Slovak National Party (Slovakia). The biggest number of seats was lost by Italy of Values-List Di Pietro (7), while the Austrian single-issue party List Dr. Martin 'lost' the largest per centage of votes (17.7 per cent) by not contesting the 2014 elections.

2: The number of countries in which no seat changed hands: Cyprus and Luxembourg. In two more member states only one seat moved from one party to another (Estonia and Malta), while in three others just two seats moved (Finland, Latvia and Netherlands). The case of the Netherlands is particularly striking, as it is a medium-sized member state with a total of 26 seats and a highly fragmented party system (see below).

Balkanized national party systems

93.4: In Malta the two biggest parties together won 93.4 per cent of the votes. The second-highest per centage, 81.3 per cent in Croatia, was the combined results of two electoral coalitions, one of two parties and one of five. In the other eleven countries in which the two biggest parties together got a majority of the votes, it was between one-half and two-third.

13: Not only has *the* biggest party become at best medium-sized, the two biggest parties together attracted a majority of the votes in just thirteen EU states (46 per cent). Moreover, in most of these 13 countries at least one of the two parties is either a current or a former electoral alliance.

6.7: The average number of parties that got MEPs elected per country. This ranges from just two in Malta to thirteen in Germany. Of the other four countries with a double-digit number of represented parties, the Netherlands was the only one without regional parties, i.e. parties with a regionally highly concentrated electorate.

2.5: The average number of parties needed to represent a majority of voters in a country. The range is from one to four with a plurality requiring three – remember that in many countries this includes at least one current or recent electoral coalition. Of the four countries that required four parties for a majority of the votes, Slovakia is the only one with a biggest party of over 20 per cent of the votes. Lithuania, on the other hand, is the only country with a biggest party of less than 20 per cent that requires just three parties.

Twisted turnout

58.2: The turnout in Greece, which was above the EU average, but shockingly low for a country that actually has *compulsory* voting (although it no longer enforces sanctions). Greece had a lower turnout than Malta, which never had compulsory voting, and Italy, which abolished compulsory voting in 1993. The two other countries with compulsory voting, Belgium and Luxembourg, still hit 90 per cent turnout.

13.0: The lowest turnout ever in a European election, recorded in Slovakia, which had a turnout of 59.1 per cent in its parliamentary election two years earlier. It was less than a third of the EU average and exactly two-third of the second-lowest turnout, which was, interestingly, in the Czech Republic.

8: The number of countries in which the biggest party gained a higher per centage of the vote than the per centage of turnout in the country. Not surprisingly, all countries were in Eastern Europe, although in two the biggest party was an electoral coalition. Slovakia had even two parties with a higher per centage of the vote than national turnout!

In the end, these numbers confirm the European trend toward highly fragmentized party systems with 2–3 medium-sized parties surrounded by 3–5 smaller parties. The multiparty systems are increasingly in flux, so much so that the two big parties change regularly. Flash parties emerge with an ever bigger bang, while party mergers have become much more significant than party splits. Even though the 2014 European elections were once again second-order elections – with big parties losing, small parties winning, and low turnout (although governmental parties seemed to have done fairly well) – these trends can be observed in first-order elections too.

The end of the big parties has so far received relatively little attention, being pushed to the sidelines by the flashier rise of new and 'extreme' parties (see Chapter 5). Its ramifications are more profound, however, at least in the short to medium term. Smaller parties lead to more difficult coalition formation processes, which can weaken government performance, and cause rising dissatisfaction and protest voting. Such processes can already be observed in Belgium and the Czech Republic, while the Netherlands requires more and more creative short-term alliances to keep its governments in power. Perhaps that should be one of the major lessons of the European elections.

Notes

1   The counting of anything in European elections or the European Parliament is a highly complex and frustrating activity. Parties change names, merge and split, or emerge into the spotlight from the amorphous 'others' category. All the presented numbers are presented in the naïve understanding that they are correct.

2   On Eastern Europe and the 2014 European elections, see Sean Hanley, 'When Anger Masks Apathy', available at http://ucl.ac.uk/european-institute/high

lights/2013-14/ep2014-cee (last visited 23 October 2015); Lee Savage, 'Hey Media! Central and East European Countries Voted in the European Elections Too . . .', *Washington Post*, 28 May 2014, available at https://www.washington post.com/news/monkey-cage/wp/2014/05/28/hey-media-central-and-east-european-countries-voted-in-the-european-parliamentary-elections-too/ (last visited 23 October 2015).

3   All election results are taken from the official website of the European Parliament: http://europarl.europa.eu/elections2014-results/en/election-results-2014.html (last visited 23 October 2014).

16 Electoral winners and political losers in the right-wing Eurosceptic camp

Elections always have many winners, and the 2014 European elections are no exception (see Chapter 15). The European People's Party (EPP) and *Spitzenkandidat* Jean-Claude Juncker claimed victory because, despite significant losses, it is still the largest political group in the European Parliament (EP). The Progressive Alliance of Socialists and Democrats (S&D) and their candidate for European Commission president Martin Schulz consider themselves winners, as they narrowed the gap with the EPP. Even the Alliance for Liberals and Democrats in Europe (ALDE) and its candidate Guy Verhofstadt, famous for living in an alternate universe, tried to reframe their historic electoral defeat as a political victory, claiming they are still kingmakers in the EP.

In sharp contrast, the media virtually unanimously declared the far right and populist Eurosceptic parties as the election winners. Even before the results were official, headlines of 'earthquakes' and 'sweeps' were being printed by an impatient press that had been foretelling 'Europe's populist backlash' for almost a year (see Chapter 5). As so often, the media interpretation was wrong, as far right parties did not win throughout Europe, and anything resembling an earthquake only took place in a couple of West European countries – as Eastern Europe was remarkably calm and uninterested.

But while the (far) right-wing Eurosceptics of the French National Front (FN) and the United Kingdom Independence Party (UKIP) were the main story in the media, it was actually the (far) left-wing Eurosceptics that were the clearest winners in terms of political groups in the EP. Driven by a victorious Syriza in Greece the United European Left/Nordic Green Left (GUE/NGL) gained ten additional seats, bringing its total MEPs to 45. With a few exceptions, including some wishful thinking by left-wing commentators, the media ignored the real successes of left-wing Eurosceptics for the, strongly exaggerated, gains of right-wing Eurosceptics.

The recently formed European Alliance for Freedom (EAF) overall won seats, but this was only because the FN made the largest gains of any political party in the elections. Overall, two parties won seats, the Austrian Freedom Party (FPÖ) and the FN, and four lost. The FN's large gains compensated for the losses of the Belgian Flemish Interest (VB), the Dutch Party for Freedom (PVV), and the Italian Northern League (LN), but could not offset the loss of representation of the Slovak National Party (SNS). Consequently, the EAF was left with more than enough seats (38 where a minimum of 25 are needed), but too few represented countries (five with a minimum of seven needed; see Chapter 6).

Similarly, while UKIP was one of the biggest winners of the 2014 European elections, its group Europe for Freedom and Democracy (EFD) gained just one seat overall. More importantly, the EFD lost representatives from several countries; most had joined the group mid-term as defectors of non-affiliated parties. Fuelled by huge losses of two of its three main members, the Czech Civic Democratic Party (ODS) and the British Conservative Party, the soft Eurosceptic European Conservatives and Reformists (ECR) lost 12 seats overall.

Political winners in the aftermath

But the electoral winners are not necessarily also the political winners of the post-election phase. Whereas in national parliamentary elections political winners are the ones that enter government, in European elections that status is based on the overall gains and losses of the political groups after the elections. Because of the particular incentive structure within the EP, individual national parties matter little, as almost all material and political rewards are related to political groups. Hence, if a group wins, its member parties win.

While surprising negotiations and moves within the right-wing Eurosceptic camp were expected prior to the elections, post-election reality has far exceeded expectations . . . and they are still ongoing. The latest rumour regarding the EAF is that they have succeeded to find their two missing partners. While still unconfirmed, several journalists have reported that the Lithuanian Order and Justice (TT) and the Polish Congress of the New Right (KNP) have joined. This would give the EAF 44 seats from seven member states. However, it will also make for a very loose and volatile political group, as KNP leader Janusz Korwin-Mikke is known as a loose canon and his ultra-liberal economics have little in common with the more protectionist economics of most other EAF parties. Moreover, his conservative views on gays and women, let alone his historical revisionism, which at least reeks of thinly veiled anti-Semitism, will conflict fundamentally with the more liberal and philo-Semitic views of Geert Wilders and the PVV.

European Tory moves

Still, the most interesting struggle is between the Tories and UKIP, in which the European multi-level game is played out in all its complexities. For both parties the European elections were, first and foremost, a bellwether for the 2015 British general elections. And UKIP defeated the Tories comprehensively in the first round. UKIP won 26.8 per cent of the vote and 24 seats, an increase of 10.7 per cent and 11 seats, while the Tories got 23.3 per cent and 19 seats, a decrease of 3.7 per cent and six seats. On the election night a boisterous Nigel Farage told his supporters (and opponents): 'you ain't seen nothing yet.' Journalists stumbled over each other to interview the new leader of the British people. No one cared about the Tories and the soft Eurosceptic ECR: the future was for the hard Eurosceptic EFD!

Just two weeks later the world looks very different. As all eyes have been on the struggling EFD and EAF, the ECR shocked everyone by building an ever-growing group in the EP. In a direct attack on UKIP, masterminded by European Tory leaders, the ECR scooped the Danish People's Party (DPP) and Finns Party (PS) from the EFD. Given that the EFD had already lost the LN to the EAF, this left UKIP with just three partners: the Czech Party of Free Citizens (Svobodní), Dutch Reformed Political Party (SGP), and Lithuanian TT. As said, the latter is rumoured to have joined the EAF, a rumour that already did the rounds well before the elections, while the SGP is said to be on its way to the ECR. Talks with Beppe Grillo of the Italian Five Star Movement (M5S) gained a lot of media attention, but seem destined to fail, as M5S has officially applied for membership in the Greens/European Free Alliance (Greens/EFA) group.

So, where the big electoral winners FN and UKIP are struggling to create or retain a political group, one of the big electoral losers, the Tories, have created the fourth biggest group in the EP. In addition to stealing the DFP and PS from the EFD, they have added five parties with one MEP each: the German Family Party, the Independent Greeks (ANEL), and the Slovak Ordinary People and Independent Personalities (OL'aNO) and New Majority (NOVA) parties. This puts the ECR at 55 MEPs, at this moment, just four less than the third-largest group ALDE.

It seems just a matter of time before ECR will overtake ALDE, as the Alternative for Germany (AfD), which gained seven, has submitted an application to join. UK Prime Minister and Tory leader David Cameron seems to fear that this could lead to tensions in the relationships with German Chancellor Angela Merkel, but might be overruled by European Tories and other ECR members. Other parties that have been eyeing the ECR are the new Bulgaria Without Censorship (BBT) with three MEPs and the Belgian nationalist New Flemish Alliance (N-VA) with four MEPs, although the latter also considers ALDE and EPP. Both parties would be an uneasy fit for the ECR, as they are not really Eurosceptic.

ECR the victor

Whether the ECR will end up as the third or fourth group in the EP, it is clear that they, and by extension the Tories, the leading party within the group, are the main political winners of the post-election period. They have significantly increased the size and, therefore, power of the ECR and, in the process, significantly weakened UKIP and possibly destroyed the EFD. There is no doubt that weakening UKIP was at least as important to the Tories as strengthening the ECR. Looking forward to the British general elections of next year, the Tories believe that UKIP is their main electoral threat. While knowing that UKIP will struggle attracting similar support in the first-order elections of 2015, they still fear a split of the right-wing/ Eurosceptic vote, with Labour the laughing third.

It looks like the Tory strategists have taken a two-staged approach to the marginalization of UKIP. By stealing the DPP and PS, the EFD is struggling for survival. This leaves UKIP with just two options. The first option is to join the *Non-Inscrits* (NI), i.e. the non-attached members who are without a political group. This would mean that UKIP would no longer be able to use its position in the EP to showcase its political relevance and its leader's significant rhetoric skills. The second option is for UKIP to be part of the EAF. This would mean that it would align itself with parties that its political competitors and (their allies in) the media consider 'extremist'. In fact, Farage himself rejected cooperation with the FN because of the party's 'anti-Semitism and general prejudice.'

But the strategy is not without risks for both the ECR and Tories. For the ECR, it will significantly undermine its group cohesion. According to VoteWatch the ECR had a group cohesion rate of 86.7 per cent in the previous EP, ranging from a low of 70.5 per cent in votes on 'regional development' to a high of 94.8 per cent in votes on 'constitutional and interinstitutional affairs.' A snapshot comparison showed that the DPP and PS had voted different from the ECR in a large number of cases.

Certain complications

For the Tories, the official alliance with parties that are often considered far right in Europe, can lead to significant critique in the UK. In fact, this has already started, both from within the more moderate wing within the party, and from political competitors. In the medium term, this could further split the Conservative Party, which will already face unprecedented internal pressures as a consequence of the planned referendum on EU membership. In the short term, it could undermine the main purpose of the whole move, marginalizing UKIP in the 2015 British elections. Because how convincing is a party warning for a 'far right' UKIP threat, when it collaborates with 'far right' Danish and Finnish parties, and former UKIP partners, in the European Parliament?

17 The key lesson from Syriza's defeat?

A different Europe requires both ideology *and* competence!

As Greek Prime Minister Alexis Tsipras is still trying to steer the almost universally disliked aGreekment through the parliament without destroying his own party, the increasingly misnamed Coalition of the Radical Left (Syriza), disappointed (ex-)supporters, and relieved pro-EU elites have started to write the narrative of Syriza's defeat. While the former continue to get stuck in externalizing guilt through toxic discourses of 'blackmail' and 'humiliation' or the broad variety of conspiracy theories surrounding #ThisIsACoup, the latter mainly argue that it was Syriza's 'radical left,' 'populist,' or 'ideological' nature that led it to fail – implying that *all* similar ideological projects are destined to fail.

Obviously, there was no 'coup' and, although many Greeks might feel genuinely 'humiliated,' they are not the 'victim' of 'blackmail.' Blackmail means 'an action, treated as a criminal offense, of demanding money from a person in return for not revealing compromising or injurious information about that person.' Not only does Greece *receive* money from the alleged blackmailers, rather than being asked to pay them, but no 'revealing compromising or injurious information' about Greece or its leaders are being threatened to be revealed. What has happened in Brussels, as happens all over the world every day, is that a strong partner has proposed a rough deal to a weak partner and has been unwilling to seriously consider any of the weak partner's arguments. The weak partner *chose* to accept that rough deal, however. There was an alternative, the Grexit, which the Greek government *chose* not to pursue. All of this was done openly, or at least as open as the opaque politics of the EU allow. One can hardly accuse German Minister of Finance Wolfgang Schäuble of being shy of expressing his preferences.

On the other side of the argument, there was little 'radical left' about Syriza's proposals regarding the softening of austerity – which find basic support among mainstream economists and other experts alike. Second, while its populism created a toxic political environment, in which Syriza opponents are attacked as 'fifth column of Germany' or 'terrorists,' most established politicians *are* professionals, who will overcome their personal dislikes if the rewards are high enough – as was made clear by the pro-Memorandum parties signing Tsipras' 'Joint Statement' and consistently voting in favor of the aGreekment in parliament. Third, the Blairist dogma that left-wing politics can only be achieved through 'pragmatism' has little empirical basis. Most notably, Blairism itself realized few left-wing goals either.

But while a radical left and populist ideology haven't helped Syriza in its negotiations with the EU, they were an indirect rather than direct cause of its ultimate failure. In fact, in a recent interview one of the most prominent and vocal (former?) Tsipras supporters, Noble Prize economist Paul Krugman, made his most accurate observation on the Greek crisis, saying rather euphemistically, 'I may have overestimated the competence of the Greek government.' You did Paul, and so did most other international fellow travellers – I tend to believe that many Greek voters didn't so much believe in Syriza's abilities to achieve change, but rather didn't see any better alternative.

Syriza failed, first and foremost, because the party and its leaders – not even speaking of its coalition partner Independent Greeks (ANEL) – were ill prepared to govern. They were willful amateurs taken to the cleaners by rigid but experienced politicians like Schäuble. Blinded by their ideology, they were convinced that their argument was absolutely right and they only needed the support of the majority of the Greek people – hence the Greferendum – to convince the rest of the EU of their superior insight.

The best example of this righteous amateurism is undoubtedly the newest darling of Europe's *gauche caviar*, Yanis Varoufakis, the now ex-Minister of Finance. In his (first of undoubtedly many) tell-all interview after resigning, with the sympathetic *New Statesman* (13 July 2015), he complained about trying to 'talk economics' in the Eurogroup but being met by a 'point blank refusal to engage in economic arguments.' Most striking of his statements, however, is his follow-up: 'And that's startling, for somebody who's used to academic debate.' As most academics who have dealt occasionally with policy makers know, politicians are not interested in long, theoretical 'lectures.' Moreover, several Eurogroup members were particularly not interested in being 'lectured to' by the person who owed them money.

Obviously, the fundamental problem of Syriza is that it made up a 'Third Way' of bailouts without austerity, which it was able to sell to a plurality of desperate Greek voters, despite it being continuously and openly rejected by the other Eurozone members. Syriza politicians knew this at least since the 2012 elections, but chose to devote all of their time criticizing the established parties and promoting their unrealistic alternative.

They did not start to lay the groundwork for possible future negotiations with the Troika.

First of all, they did not develop at least a rudimentary plan for a fallback option, i.e. a Grexit. Varoufakis recently claimed that they only debated some alternative measures on the night of the Greferendum – oh irony – but that he couldn't convince his inner-circle colleagues of their feasibility. Even if it is true that Tsipras and others approached a slew of non-EU countries – China, Iran and Russia – in 2014, to secure funding for a possible Grexit, this hardly counts as preparation of a fallback option. Rather, the fact that they seriously thought that, most notably, Russia would be able and willing to bankroll a Grexit – as it struggles through an economic crisis of its own as well as EU and US sanctions – is painful proof of their lack of understanding of the international political context.

Second, and even more important, Syriza failed to muster international support for its preferred alternative. As we learned from the recent negotiations, French and Italian social democrats were open to a softening of the austerity conditions. But rather than reaching out to possible mainstream allies, particularly in other hard-hit countries, Syriza politicians criticized several Southern European countries for their handling of the crisis and debt. Its key strategy seems to have been to wait for other 'radical left' parties to come to power in Southern Europe and then to collectively renegotiate the Memorandum. The obvious problem was one of sequencing. Greece *had* to negotiate its deals well before the other countries held elections – leaving aside the fact that there were few indications that other radical left parties would become the dominant party in a new government.

Consequently, when Tsipras met his counterparts in Brussels, he had no real allies or fallback option. It was only then, under extreme public and time pressure, that he tried to sell his alternative to the other European leaders. When they called his bluff, he couldn't threaten with a Grexit, and instead went for 'a democratic mandate.' But while the 'no' vote in the Greferendum took most Eurogroup leaders by surprise, it obviously didn't really affect their position. After all, their own democratic mandates come from their own voters, and in many countries the voters were far from sympathetic to the Greek plight. Note, for example, that Tsipras' current approval rating of roughly 60 per cent is more than matched by Schäuble's 70 per cent – not to speak of the fact that there are almost eight times more Germans than Greeks.

Consequently, the most important broader lesson to learn is not that 'a different Europe' is necessarily impossible – although it is debatable that it is possible within the EU. But whether inside or outside of the EU, *if* a different Europe is indeed possible, it can only be achieved by competent, well-prepared politicians. This is not to say that they have to be mainstream or even professional politicians; in fact, several Syriza members are professional politicians and/or come from the mainstream (e.g. PASOK). Politicians who want to create a different Europe have to accept, however reluctantly, that politics is a profession with specific rules and skills. To achieve anything in politics, including changing the rules, you have to master 'the art of the possible,' as conservative German statesman Otto von Bismarck famously said, rather than merely trumpet 'the truth.'

18 It's time to end the Eurosceptic illusions!

Anyone (still) following the 'Greek crisis' in the social and traditional media will have noticed the growing expressions of Euroscepticism. What once was a minor nuisance in the European Union (EU), relegated to mostly ostracized extreme and radical parties, is rapidly becoming the predominant sentiment across Europe, whatever the position on the EU–Greece negotiations (see Chapter 12).

The term 'Euroscepticism' has always been a container concept, initially denoting anyone who had *some* critique on 'The European Project,' however small or detailed. This was not very problematic until the late 1980s, as European integration was still an elite-driven process profiting from a 'permissive consensus' of the vast majority of the European peoples. The Maastricht Treaty of 1992 changed this, slowly but steadily. It did not only introduce the EU and the (now increasingly cursed) Euro, but also birthed mass Euroscepticism. Sure, it took some time, but by the late 1990s Euroscepticism was so diverse and widespread, at both the elite and mass levels, that scholars like British political scientists Aleks Szczerbiak and Paul Taggart started to distinguish between 'soft' and 'hard' Euroscepticism, in which the former referred to detailed critique and the latter to more fundamental criticism.[1]

My colleague Petr Kopecký and I elaborated upon this important innovation by going to the core of the process of European integration and distinguishing between general and specific critique/support of European integration.[2] By *diffuse* critique we meant criticism of the general *ideas* of European integration that underlie the EU, i.e. pooled sovereignty and an integrated market. By *specific* critique we denoted criticism of the general *practice* of European integration; i.e. the EU as it *is* and as it is developing. We reserved Euroscepticism, in line with the more general meaning of the term 'scepticism,' for views that are supportive of the ideas of European integration, but critique its general practice (i.e. the EU). We termed critique of both the general practice *and* the general ideas Eurorejects, as they reject the fundamentals of the process of European integration.

The rise of Euroscepticism is not so much a consequence of changed values or priorities of the European masses, but rather of the changed nature of the process of European integration and the increasing awareness of this by the European elites and masses. Today's EU is a very different beast than the European (Economic) Community of the 1980s. Moreover, the Great Recession has finally hit home what 'integration' and 'solidarity' really mean, and many Europeans don't like it. Still, both at the elite and mass level most responses are as halfhearted and misdirected as the EU solutions to the Greek crisis and Great Recession. Consequently, although there is a minor increase in Eurorejection too – notably in the French Front National and Dutch Party for Freedom (see Chapter 6), most elites and masses have responded with some vague form of Euroscepticism.

The most extreme example of this conflicted response to the perceived fallacies of the EU is that of the current Greek government, which literally made its career by selling an illusionary 'Third Way' in between the politics of the Memorandum – mainly supported by New Democracy (ND) and Panhellenic Socialist Movement (PASOK) – and the Grexit – chiefly supported by the Communist Party of Greece (KKE) and Golden Dawn (XA). By now the last illusions of this misguided policy should be clear to all, particularly those manipulated into voting 'OXI' (no) in the Greferendum, while experts are left to calculate the enormous economic and political costs that this half year of amateur-politics of Tsipras and Varoufakis has cost Greece (see Chapter 18).

Just as the Greek parties and people continue to reject a Grexit, instead complaining about the 'EU dictatorship' and 'German blackmail,' the vast majority of non-centrist parties of left and right keep hiding behind a socially more acceptable, but politically disingenuous, Euroscepticism. From most members of the right-wing Eurosceptic European Conservatives and Reformists (ECR) group to the majority in the left-wing Eurosceptic European United Left – Nordic Green Left (GUE-NGL) group the official mantra remains that 'A Different Europe is Possible' within the EU. It is not!

The core principles of the process of European integration, of which the EU is the current representation, are and will always be: pooled sovereignty and an integrated market. In other words, the EU is inherently a transnational neoliberal project! Sovereignists of the right (and left) as well as (real) social democrats and socialists on the left should therefore be fundamentally opposed to the EU. It is unrealistic to expect, and disingenuous to suggest, that the EU can be transformed into anything else – leaving aside a couple of 'green', 'national', and 'social' tweaks here and there. Anything else is *by definition* not the EU. There is therefore no reason to 'reform' the EU into a 'European of Nations' or a 'Europe of International Solidarity.' In fact, this can *only* be achieved outside of the EU!

As politicians like Greek Prime Minister Tsipras know very well, there currently is no majority support for an exit in any EU member state, not even in Greece or the United Kingdom. But rather than continuing to sell an illusion, sovereignist politicians of the left and right should shed their deceiving Euroscepticism, which in the end only strengthens the idea that the EU is the (only) way forward, and start developing a true *alternative* to life in the EU. They should explain to their supporters that what they want to achieve, cannot be realized within the confinements of the EU, and why an exit does not equate to a Third World War or Auschwitz (see Chapter 13). Obviously, this goes beyond simplistic studies such as the Nexit report of the PVV in the Netherlands. Politicians will have to be honest about the probable short-term costs that will almost certainly have to be paid for the possible long-term gains.

In short, they have to show that a different Europe is possible, but not within this EU or any future EU. Any party or political group that wants to build a really different 'Europe' will have to do so *outside* of the EU. But in order to do so, they will have to denounce their official Euroscepticism and start convincing the population to do the same. Even if this will not convince a majority of Europeans, it will lead to a more honest and transparent debate on European integration. And this will benefit everyone, irrespective of their position on the EU.

Notes

1   See, among others, Aleks Szczerbiak and Paul Taggart (eds), *Opposing Europe? The Comparative Party Politics of Euroscepticism*. Oxford: Oxford University Press, 2008, 2 Volumes.
2   Petr Kopecký and Cas Mudde, 'The Two Sides of Euroscepticism. Party Positions on European Integration in East Central Europe', *European Union Politics*, Vol. 3, No. 3, 2002, pp. 297–326.

19 'Weimar Greece' and the future of Europe

At least since the 2012 parliamentary elections, in both May and June, Greece has been the European country to invoke the most dire predictions for the future. Although far right parties have gained three to four times as much electoral support in other European countries, the roughly six per cent of the vote for the, until then unknown, Golden Dawn (XA) party has unleashed hordes of journalists on the crisis-ridden country – hopefully compensating at least for some of the lost tourism income – and have put commentators into a frenzy. Mostly asking rhetoric questions, like 'is fascism back in Europe?,' (self-)proclaimed experts from all over the globe hark back to the inevitable trauma of Weimar Germany to 'explain' the current situation in Greece. Some even went as far as to claim that the 'Weimar on the Agean' is the future of all of Europe!

The idea is simple: economic crisis breeds frustration that leads to the support for anti-democratic parties (see also Chapter 3). After all, wasn't it the Great Depression that created Adolf Hitler? Yes, to an extent it was, although Hitler never achieved more than one-third of the vote and his ascent to power was made possible by naïve and opportunistic behavior of the political establishment. More importantly, that same Great Depression did not lead to extreme right parties coming to power through elections in other countries. In other words, Weimar Germany was the exception, not the rule.

So, has the Great Recession created a Weimar Greece and, if so, is this the exception in or the (future) of Europe? At first sight the answer seems an easy 'no.' Truly extremist parties of right and left received a total of about 12 per cent of the vote in the January 2015 elections: Golden Dawn got 6.3 per cent and the Communist Party of Greece (KKE) 5.5 per cent. That said, populist parties gained more than 40 per cent in total: notably, the Coalition of the Radical Left (Syriza) gained 36.6 per cent and the Independent Greeks (ANEL) 4.8 per cent. While populists oppose certain features of *liberal* democracy, they do accept the basic tenets of democracy (see Chapter 11). In conclusion, the main parties supporting liberal democracy received only a minority of the votes; in fact, in the current parliament pro-liberal democracy parties hold just 106 of the 300 seats![1] In other words, whereas Weimar Germany was a democracy without democrats, contemporary Greece is a liberal democracy without liberal democrats.

There is another similarity between Weimar Germany and contemporary (Weimar) Greece: they are the exception, not the rule (see also Chapter 10). Just as the Great Depression didn't lead to a continental rise of fascist parties, the Great Recession has not given way to a Europe-wide upsurge in support for far right parties. On top of that, Golden Dawn is the only clearly extreme right party to gain, albeit modestly. Strikingly, all four other 'bailout countries' have no significant far right party – Golden Dawn's little Cypriot cousin, the National Popular Front (ELAM), is the most successful with a mere 1.1 per cent in the 2011 parliamentary elections and 2.7 per cent in the 2014 European elections. In fact, if the bailout countries have seen any broader electoral response, and even this is limited to a few countries, it is the implosion of the established parties, most notably of the centre-left, and the rise of left-wing populist parties (see also Chapter 15).

It is in this respect that Greece again stands out. Syriza shot from 4.6 per cent in 2007 to 36.3 per cent in January 2015, while the mainstream left-wing Panhellenic Socialist Movement (PASOK) crashed from 43.9 per cent in 2009 to a measly 4.7 per cent in 2015. So far this is unique to Greece, but recent polls in Spain show that the left-wing populist party We Can (Podemos) could be set for a similar trajectory, although both the rise of Podemos and the implosion of the mainstream left-wing Spanish Socialist Workers' Party (PSOE) are less extreme. And while Italy has seen the meteoric rise of a more or less left-wing populist upstart, the Five Star Movement (M5S) of comedian Beppe Grillo, this has been accompanied by a rather modest decrease of the mainstream left-wing Democratic Party (PD). In fact, Italy has seen a more pronounced implosion of support for the mainstream and radical right populist parties, Forza Italia (FI) and the Lega Nord (LN).

In short, Greece isn't Europe and Europe isn't Greece. In a strict sense contemporary Greece is also not the same as Weimar Germany, as the main challenge comes from anti-liberal democratic populists instead of anti-democratic extremists. That said, there are important similarities. Just as Weimar Germany was a democracy without democrats, Greece is a liberal democracy without liberal democrats. But while Weimar Germany was a state in perpetual crisis, Greece has gone through substantial periods of economic and political stability. But, as Greek political scientist Takis Pappas has forcefully argued, the political establishment never truly developed a liberal democratic regime in Greece.[2] Andreas Papandreou made PASOK into a left-wing populist party, rather than a more traditional West

European social democratic one, and established a powerful clientelist party-state. Its main right-wing competitor, New Democracy (ND), has copied PASOK's clientelist approach to the state, but not its populist approach to politics.

In other words, the Great Recession has not turned Greece into an illiberal democracy, or (more positively formulated) an ill-functioning liberal democracy; it has always been one. Similarly, the economic crisis has not strengthened political extremism, as Greece has always had a relatively strong extremist party in the pro-Soviet KKE. As far as Greek politics has been transformed, it is in the replacement of the establishment left-wing populist PASOK by the upstart left-wing populist Syriza. How significant that transformation is for Greek (liberal) democracy, will become clear in the coming months and years.

Notes

1 The situation changed only marginally in the parliamentary elections of September 2015, in which liberal democratic parties gained a total of 112 seats: New Democracy 75, PASOK-DIMAR 17, Potami 11 and EK 9.
2 See, most notably, Takis Pappas, *Populism and Crisis Politics in Greece.* New York: Palgrave Macmillan, 2014; and 'Why Greece Failed', *Journal of Democracy*, Vol. 24, No. 2, 2013, pp. 31–45.

20 Portugal faces a political crisis, but it's the same one facing governments everywhere

2015 has not been a good year for Europe. If one is to believe social media, it has been a year of 'crises' and 'coups.' The first half of the year was dominated by 'the Greek crisis,' which after a referendum and an alleged coup led to a third bailout for Greece. As soon as that was settled, Europe entered 'the refugee crisis,' which is still ongoing. Alongside that we've seen the rise of far right parties, both traditional ones like the Austrian Freedom Party (FPÖ) and Swiss People's Party (SVP), and new ones, like Hungarian Prime Minister Viktor Orbán's Fidesz-Hungarian Civic Alliance (see Chapter 6), and possibly Poland's Jaroslaw Kaczynski's Law and Justice (PiS) party, the big winner of the weekend's elections.

Amidst this crisis and change, Portugal has been an exception. It was hard hit by the economic crisis and austerity measures that came alongside the country's 2011 bailout by the European Union (EU) and International Monetary Fund (IMF). But no strong left or right populist party emerged. Portugal's recent parliamentary elections saw only modest gains for 'radical' parties.

Consequently, Portugal remained the forgotten child in Southern Europe, crowded out by the more tumultuous politics in Greece, Italy and Spain. Until last week.

Here are the election results

Portugal held elections, as scheduled, on 4 October. To the surprise of many, Prime Minister Pedro Passos Coelho's right-wing bloc 'Portugal Ahead' of the misnamed Social Democratic Party (PPD-PSD) and the CDS-People's Party (CDS-PP) remained the largest party in the *Assembleia da República* with 107 of the 230 seats in the parliament. However, Portugal Ahead lost 24 seats, whereas the opposition Socialist Party (PS) came second with 86 seats, an increase of 12. The biggest winner was the radical Left Bloc (BE), more than doubling its number of seats from eight to 19, while the radical left Unitary Democratic Union (CDU), a coalition between the Portuguese

Communist Party (PCP) and the Ecologist Party 'The Greens' (PEV), gained one additional seat, bringing its total also to 19. Finally, the animal rights party People-Animals-Nature (PAN) entered parliament for the first time with one seat.

Socialist leader Antonio Costa claimed to have the support of a parliamentary majority for a triple-left coalition government among his centre-left PS and the more radical BE and CDU. But Portugal's president Anibal Cavaco Silva instead turned to conservative premier Coelho, who was only able to form a minority government.

Then came social media's overreaction

The reaction in social media and the more extreme corners of the news media was extreme. 'Eurozone crosses Rubicon as Portugal's anti-euro left banned from power,' headlined the British right-wing Eurosceptic *The Telegraph*. Its point of view was echoed by Eurosceptic darlings of the right, such as the British conservative Member of the European Parliament Daniel Hannan, and left, like *Guardian* columnist Owen Jones.

Many on social media called it a 'coup,' just as when Greek premier Alexis Tsipras was 'forced' into the third bailout – which led to the trending of #ThisIsACoup on Twitter. But all this was sensationalizing.

First, as the British political scientist Chris Hanretty explained in an excellent column,[1] this decision is perfectly legal and within the president's constitutional powers. In the Portuguese semi-presidential system, the president has the prerogative to 'appoint the Prime Minister after consulting the parties with seats in Assembly of the Republic and in the light of the electoral results' (Art. 187). It is further perfectly logical that the leader of the largest faction in parliament gets the first stab at forming a government, although it is less common that a minority government would be chosen when a majority government is possible. Second, there is no evidence that the European Union helped keep the Eurosceptic left in Portugal from power.

One thing did stand out: the official justification President Silva gave for his decision. He referred to the left-wing parties as 'anti-European forces' and stated:

> This is the worst moment for a radical change to the foundations of our democracy. (. . .) After we carried out an onerous programme of financial assistance, entailing heavy sacrifices, it is my duty, within my constitutional powers, to do everything possible to prevent false signals being sent to financial institutions, investors and markets.

With this statement the president sent a strong signal to socialist leader Costa to join a coalition with (under!) premier Coelho and continue the austerity measures – or be excluded from political power.

But there is a real political crisis – and it's a common one

And yet Silva's statement has thrown Portugal into a political crisis. Coelho has the support of the president but not of the parliament. Costa has the support of the parliament but not of the president. Unfortunately, within Portugal's semi-presidential system, a prime minister needs the support of both.

The Portuguese political crisis is a perfect example of the tension between 'responsiveness' and 'responsibility' that the late Irish political scientist Peter Mair discussed in his posthumous book *Ruling the Void: The Hollowing of Western Democracy.*[2] As had many politicians before him, President Silva had to choose between being 'responsive' to the Portuguese electorate and 'responsible' to the domestic and international business community. This tension has intensified in our interconnected world, in which many countries have, wittingly or unwittingly, surrendered part of their national sovereignty to international and supranational organizations.

This tension is strongest in the EU, and particularly within the Eurozone, but also exists in other regions of the world, often as a consequence of loans by the IMF and the World Bank.

The tension between responsiveness and responsibility faces governments worldwide

The tension between responsiveness and responsibility is feeding political dissatisfaction around the world, which has lead to the rise of old and new political challengers. In many cases, these challengers present themselves as political outsiders and use a populist discourse, exalting the people and demonizing the elite. Domestic and foreign elites attack them as 'irresponsible,' an accusation they often claim as a badge of honor. The challengers promise to give the power back to the people – or, in other words, to put responsiveness over responsibility.

The most extreme recent example is undoubtedly the late Venezuelan president Hugo Chávez, who started a frontal attack on the 'responsible politics' of the so-called Washington Consensus, a program of neoliberal economic development and market reforms closely tied to the IMF and World Bank. His critique of US capitalism and foreign policy, in his eyes enforced by the IMF and World Bank, found support among several other left-wing populist presidents in the region – most notably, Evo Morales in Bolivia, Rafael Correa in Ecuador and Daniel Ortega in Nicaragua. All of them promised to put the interests of their own people over the demands of the 'responsible' institutions of global finance.

While many European challengers have promised this in campaigns, few have had the power to do so, as the parliamentary system forces them into coalitions with more responsible parties. The notable exception is Greece, where a coalition of populist parties came to power at the beginning of the year.

What happens when even populists choose responsibility?

So what happens when populists come to power – and then succumb to responsibility? That's what happened in Greece, earlier this year, when left-wing populist premier Tsipras ignored the majority of the Greek people, who had voted against austerity in the 'Greferendum.' Under huge international pressure, Tsipras signed the 'Agreekment,' which included a third bailout and ongoing austerity.

Greece's September elections, which returned Tsipras to power, weren't a real test yet. Tspiras called elections before the Greek people were confronted with the consequences of the bailout. Opposition parties were still in disarray. The next elections, undoubtedly within a year or two, will show whether voters go back to voting for responsibility (i.e. the conservative New Democracy party) or even further to responsiveness, with an old or new political 'outsider' promising the impossible.

Notes

1   'Dan Hannan and Owen Jones Are Both Wrong on Portugal', available at https://medium.com/@chrishanretty/dan-hannan-and-owen-jones-are-both-wrong-on-portugal-6c3e38b9a5e8#.bfpgmty26 (last visited 29 October 2015).
2   Peter Mair, *Ruling the Void: The Hollowing of Western Democracy*. London: Verso, 2013.

Part IV

Liberal democracy

21 The intolerance of the tolerant

The entry of the Sweden Democrats into the Swedish parliament after the elections of 19 September 2010 means that Europe's last 'bastion of tolerance' has fallen.[1] When radical right parties were making significant electoral gains elsewhere in the 1980s and 1990s, voters in the traditional liberal countries of northern Europe – such as Denmark, the Netherlands and Sweden – were resistant to their claims. Now the first two are among the most accommodating of intolerance: the Danish People's Party (DPP) of Pia Kjærsgaard has been a solid supporter of right-wing minority governments in Denmark since 2001, while the Party for Freedom (PVV) of Geert Wilders has played a similar role in the Netherlands between 2010 and 2012.

But is it really the case that the former 'bastions of tolerance' have become as intolerant (or even more so) than other European countries; and, if so, why did it take them so long? Or is there something else at play?

A closer look at the results of research into European citizens' attitudes suggests a more complex and interesting picture. Most such surveys show Denmark, the Netherlands and Sweden still to be among the most tolerant countries in Europe – and, by extension, the world.

Traditionally, the populations of northern Europe have been most in favour of gay rights and gender equality. Eurobarometer 66 (2006) showed that the Netherlands, Sweden, and Denmark topped the EU-25 in terms of popular support for gay marriage (between 82 and 69 per cent), while the Netherlands and Sweden were the only two countries where a majority supported that 'adoption of children should be authorized for homosexual couples throughout Europe' – Denmark and Austria had the third-highest support with 44 per cent. Special Barometer 428 (2015) found very high support for modern gender conceptions and for gender equality in the northern European countries. For example, only in Denmark, Finland, Netherlands and Sweden a majority of the population disagree with the statement 'all in all family life suffers when the mother has a full time job,' while a majority of the population in Denmark, Netherlands, and Sweden 'totally disagreed' that 'overall men are less competent than women to perform household tasks.' The three were also among the five EU member states with the highest per centages of people that 'totally agree' that 'equality between men and women is a fundamental right.'

Regarding the broad value of 'tolerance,' a Eurobarometer poll of 2000, admittedly conducted before the most recent far right advances and European Union (EU) enlargements, found that an average of 14 per cent of populations across the EU were classified as intolerant – higher than in the Netherlands (11 per cent) and Sweden (nine per cent), but lower than in Denmark (20 per cent). In addition, these countries scored high on the index of those judged to be either 'passively' or 'actively' tolerant: against an EU average of 60 per cent, Sweden scored 76 per cent (just below the highest, Spain), and Denmark recorded 64 per cent.

A more recent Eurobarometer (71/2010) confirmed the continued tolerance in northern Europe. Asked whether other ethnic groups 'enrich the cultural life' of their country, 80 per cent of Swedes, 66 per cent of Dutch, and 65 per cent of Danes tended to agree – only one other country, Finland, was in the top-4 of this list. This was also the case with regard to the question whether 'immigrants can play an important role in developing greater understanding and tolerance with the rest of the world' – here the per centages that tended to agree were 77 (Sweden and Finland), 69 (Denmark), and 65 (Netherlands). Finally, the three countries were all in the top-6 of EU member states in terms of per centage of people that tended to agree that 'the arrival of immigrants in Europe can be effective in solving the problem of Europe's ageing population.'

Against this, there is some evidence that Denmark and the Netherlands at least do stand out in terms of negative attitudes towards Muslims – though, regrettably, there are few relevant surveys that include any of the three countries under scrutiny. Already in 2000, i.e. before the terrorist attacks of 9/11, the Dutch were among the least tolerant towards Muslim immigrants within the EU. Of the 15 EU member states of that time, Sweden was the most open to new Muslims immigrants, Denmark fourth, and the Netherlands ranked twelfth. However, the Dutch were barely more accepting towards new East European immigrants, while the Danes and Swedes were. Interestingly, the three countries had the highest per centages of people that tended to agree with the statement, 'In schools where there are too many children from these minority groups, the quality of education suffers.'

More recently, one Pew survey (2005) ranked the Dutch among the most anti-Muslim on some indicators – Denmark and Sweden were not included in the study. Although Dutch anti-Islam sentiments were most striking in contrast to their very high pro-Christianity and pro-Judaism sentiments, the

Dutch had the highest percentage of people believing that Islam 'is prone to violence' and one of the highest levels of support among European countries for banning head scarves. But another Pew survey of the same year had the Netherlands in the middle of a group of six European countries with regard to prejudices towards Muslims – other countries were France, Germany, Great-Britain, Poland, and Spain. Still, a slight majority of Dutch people had an 'unfavourable' view of Muslims, 51 per cent versus 45 per cent 'favourable,' and 65 per cent thought that Muslims 'want to remain distinct.'

In addition, both the European Commission against Racism and Intolerance (ECRI) and the European Monitoring Centre on Racism and Xenophobia (EUMC) have singled out the Netherlands (and to a lesser extent Denmark) for their Islamophobic political and public climate. A 2012 ECRI report criticizes both the media and 'some politicians' for continuing 'to portray Muslims in a negative light' and 'strongly recommends that the authorities encourage debate within the media on the image which they convey of Islam and Muslim communities.' An earlier ECRI report (2007) had spoken about a 'dramatic deterioration' in the tone of Dutch political and public debate about integration and issues related to ethnic minorities.

These (admittedly partial) findings indicate that the alleged former bastions of tolerance in fact are still tolerant – just not toward Muslims. Moreover, in this particular intolerance toward a religious group they outdo generally less tolerant other European countries. Why?

A possible explanation, counterintuitive as it might seem, is that it is *because* of their overall social tolerance – rather than despite it – that these countries have become among the most openly Islamophobic. The logic of the argument is threefold, relating to nationalism, conformism, and tolerance itself.

First, in all three countries tolerance was closely associated with a negative attitude toward ethnic nationalism and a self-perception of being that allegedly unique thing, a 'non-nationalist nation.' In part because of the particular way the countries dealt with their experience of the Second World War, nationalism was linked almost intrinsically with Nazism and the Holocaust. Hence, ethnic-national discourses, let alone racial ones, were suspect, and shunned by all but the ostracised extreme right. So, whereas radical right parties in countries such as Austria, Belgium, or France could relate their anti-immigrant struggle to more broadly shared national narratives, this option was not available in Denmark, the Netherlands or Sweden.

Second, most everyday citizens in these countries self-identified as tolerant, and would in any case self-censor where this was felt necessary; but in addition, their elite had a special weapon at their disposal in its struggle to keep politics 'politically correct' – conformity. After all, northern Europe is as well known for its tolerance as for its conformity, which traditionally includes a high trust in state actors and institutions. The often genuinely pro-multicultural elites were able to keep the immigration issue off the agenda, because the most intolerant people were also the most conformist.

Third, the countries under scrutiny – Denmark, the Netherlands and Sweden – and their close neighbours have traditionally been, and still are, among the most tolerant in Europe, particularly regarding issues such as women's rights and gay rights. In addition, they are among Europe's least religious societies, with a dominant secular majority and the formerly influential religious interests now politically marginalised. In this context, it is easy to construct Islam as a threat both to the national way of life and to liberal democracy as it is understood in these countries.

The argument is twofold. First, after decades of secularisation, Islam is a (rapidly) growing religion that threatens the secular consensus by bringing religious issues back onto the public agenda. Second, (orthodox) Islam – and vocal Muslims – openly challenge local beliefs on gender equality and gay rights, which are regarded as fundamental aspects of liberal democracy in these countries. Hence, it is the tolerant liberal democrats who oppose the intolerant Muslims.

The implication is that the recent rise of anti-Islam sentiment in northern Europe is proof neither of the end of tolerance in Europe nor of the Europeanisation of ethnic nationalism. It is instead an outpouring of the intolerance of the tolerant, long (self-)censored by a political culture of anti-nationalism and conformity. The fact that (orthodox) Muslims can be opposed with a liberal democratic discourse, rather than an ethnic-nationalist one, makes it at last politically acceptable, and increasingly politically correct, to express ethnic prejudice in these countries.

Note

1   This text is based on the Einaudi Chair Lecture, given by the author at Cornell University on 19 October 2012.

22 After the storms

Time to go beyond the obvious responses

In the past weeks Europe has been violently pointed to the still growing tensions in its ever more multi-ethnic societies. On 22 July a Norwegian extreme right terrorist detonated a bomb in the downtown of the nation's capital of Oslo, killing eight people, and then went to the small island of Utøya, and shot a staggering 69 members of the youth organization of the social democratic party, which held a gathering on the island. While not nearly as deadly, the August 2011 riots in London, and some other English cities, sent a shockwave through many European countries too. In just a couple of days at least four people were killed, millions of pounds of property was destroyed, and over three thousand people were arrested.

Unlike during the riots in France in 2005, most media didn't use terms like 'race riots' or link the unrest to Islam and young Muslims – undoubtedly also a result of the embarrassing early linkage of the Norway bombing to alleged Jihadists in many western media. They did put the riots in the broader perspective of a failed politics of multiculturalism, as prominent politicians like British Prime Minister David Cameron, French President Nicolas Sarkozy, and German Chancellor Angela Merkel had recently proclaimed. Reactions of commentators and politicians to both events have been largely predictable, and inconsequential, although some worrying trends are visible.

The (far) right responded to the Norwegian tragedy with unanimous condemnation of the act ... but not the motivations. In fact, various 'counterjihadist' authors, like Oslo-based American author Bruce Bawer, and right-wing populist politicians, such as Norwegian Progress Party leader Siv Jensen, used the opportunity to condemn the shooter as a madman and at the same time echo his main concerns of an alleged Islamization of Europe. Some almost went as far as to suggest that this was both an irrational response to, and a logical consequence of, the 'failed' multiculturalist politics of the mainstream (left-wing) parties. In other words, while the violence was, of course, not to be condoned, they did understand why the shooter had become so frustrated and why he felt so powerless to resort to violence.

The (far) left obviously came to different conclusions. They saw the shooter as the logical consequence of increasing Islamophobia in the (right-wing) media and political debate. Hence, rather than a madman, or 'lone wolf,' he was the creation of insidious political forces, which should be stopped. In addition to calling for an increased vigilance toward the 'far right' in general, including political parties, they demanded a more civil debate on multiculturalism and a more tolerant policy towards immigrants and minorities. Some even went so far as to call for the state monitoring of far right chat rooms and websites and for increased censorship of the Internet. This again led to some strong reactions from the (radical) right, who spoke of a 'witch hunt' and 'Soviet-style state repression.'

How different was the reaction to the English riots? At times with racist undertones, right-wing commentators and politicians responded with familiar authoritarianism and elitism to the riots. Blaming the youth's nihilist 'yob culture,' and sometimes even 'black culture,' on the 'cultural relativism' of the left, they called for a 'zero tolerance' response with massive police force – some even wanted the army to be deployed. And, responding to the reported role of direct messaging and social media among rioters, they called for a strict censorship and monitoring of both. Prime Minister Cameron even hinted at a ban on social media sites like Facebook and Twitter.

Now it was the turn of the left to play the role of defender of freedom and liberty. Seeing the riots mainly in terms of socio-economic deprivation and racism, they blamed the (right-wing) authorities for police discrimination, media sensationalism, and anti-social politics, which have created an underclass devoid of chances or hope. While violence was obviously not the answer, they understood that these poor youths would feel so frustrated and powerless that they saw no other option than to resort to it.

But neither the Norwegian tragedy nor the English riots are 'logical' consequences of Europe's multi-ethnic society and the alleged failure of 'multicultural politics' – whatever that actually means. Although neither event might be unique, they are the work of only a tiny part of large groups of dissatisfied people. For very different reasons, a large and ever growing group of Europeans are fed up with politicians from both sides of the political spectrum and the way they have shaped, or failed to shape, their societies. Neither group is homogeneous and, hence, it is impossible to listen to 'their voice.' The Norwegian terrorist drew upon a broad range of ideological positions and political camps, many of which hate each other as much as they hate Muslim immigrants, and the British rioters pitted black against Asian, black against white, white against Asian, etc. While the origins were local and fairly well defined – police harassment, racism, unemployment – the riots soon spread to areas and involved people who had little to do with these phenomena.

Hence, the responses to these events should be as complex as the frustrations underlying them. Moreover, they should be based on thorough police investigation and scientific research – clearly identifying causes, concerns, and consequences – rather than on media mania and spur of the moment crisis management. Censorship and state encroachment on citizen's privacy should be absolute last resort measures, only to be discussed if everything else has failed. Rather than further muzzling the voices of the frustrated, European societies need truly open debates, in which all voices are heard, and political elites finally dare to develop and defend well-grounded policies to shape their multi-ethnic societies. It should be clear to all involved that every society has tensions, and developing multi-ethnic societies might even have more of them. No one policy will make everyone happy, but no policy at all makes no one happy!

23 Norway's democratic example

The verdict of 24 August 2012 in the case of Norway's most (in)famous citizen, the extreme right terrorist Anders Breivik, has provoked a lot of confusion and rage – mostly outside the country itself. The defendant killed seventy-seven people on 22 July 2011 in a bombing in Oslo and a shooting on the nearby island of Utøya, by far the deadliest terrorist attack in Norwegian history and one of the deadliest in European history (see Chapter 22).

Yet, to the dismay of many foreigners, he was sentenced to 'only' twenty-one years in prison, which is the effective judicial extent of 'life imprisonment' in Norway. What many of these observers miss – although I doubt it will temper their anger – is the probability that Breivik will serve much longer than twenty-one years as part of a further period of 'preventative detention.'

While Breivik's verdict was met with approval and relief in most of Norway, commentators around the world proclaimed that the killer had won. In a hyperbolically titled article in *The Telegraph* – 'Anders Breivik's Sordid Victory Is Complete' (24 August 2012) – Dan Hodges claimed that 'Anders Behring Breivik declared war on humanity. And he won.' In the usually more measured pages of *Foreign Policy* (24 August 2012), Elias Groll, too, argued that 'Breivik Won' because, 'In the end, Norway's killer got what he wanted: official recognition that his extremist ideology doesn't make him a madman.'

Perhaps these arguments make sense according to a vision of justice in which the main aim of convictions is retaliation. Fortunately, Norway doesn't subscribe to this backward view. Its judicial system sentences people on the basis of their crimes and in hope of their rehabilitation. The idea behind limiting a life-sentence to a maximum of twenty-one years' imprisonment is that this is a very long period during which a person can change fundamentally. If, however, this doesn't happen, the sentence can be extended, as part of so-called preventative detention.

Moreover, the Norwegian court did not consider Breivik mentally insane, making this judgment on the basis of an evaluation of his mental situation rather than his political ideology. A true liberal democracy outlaws actions, not ideas (see also Chapter 24) – in contrast to totalitarian systems, which brand certain ideas as insane and/or criminal. Clearly, the Norwegian court and the larger society reject Breivik's ideology, but his ideological views do not constitute the basis of his crime or of his (in)sanity.

In the end, the Norwegian court came to the only possible verdict in this case. It ruled that Breivik, although suffering from 'an inflated sense of self,' was legally responsible for his actions and guilty of a hideous crime. In addition, Norwegian society responded to Breivik's horrific acts in the best way possible. It neither called for increased repressive measures, in a feeble attempt to create the illusion of a totally safe society, nor did it go on a witch-hunt against Breivik and people with similar thoughts. Instead, the society turned inward, analysed what had driven Breivik to his terrible deed, and decided that its ideals were still worth standing up for.

Hence, Norwegian politicians did not sacrifice liberty and justice in the fight against terrorism, in sharp contrast to earlier responses to terrorism in, for example, the Netherlands – after the killings of Pim Fortuyn in 2002 and Theo van Gogh in 2004 – or the United States – after the attacks of 9/11. They did not increase repression without providing any evidence for its effectiveness. From the outset, Norway's Prime Minister Jens Stoltenberg declared his unwavering support for liberal democracy and for a multicultural society, and lived up to his words. The government did introduce some measured security reforms, but focused primarily on making Norway more rather than less liberal.

Stoltenberg said, in an interview with *The Telegraph* (21 July 2012):

> [Breivik] managed to cause lots of sorrow and damage, and many people will live with the wounds, but he failed in his main project, which was to change Norway, to make Norway less open, less tolerant. [. . .] Because we have become actually the opposite, and in that way our democratic society won.

Thus, Norwegians and their prime minister alike understood that the most important qualities needed in responding to the terrorist attack were: to help the victims, not punish the perpetrator; to explain why society is from time to time at risk of attack by extremists, not claim to be able to create a 100 per cent safe society; to reach out to the targeted communities and ensure that they are fully-fledged members of society, not treat them as potential causes of concern; and to strengthen the core of the political system, not sacrifice some of its core values.

All that is why, unlike in so many other cases, this time, in Norway, the terrorist lost and liberal democracy won. It can only be hoped that, in the likely event of a future terrorist attack (from whatever extremist group), the citizens and leaders of other liberal democracies will recall the Norwegian response and learn the right lessons.

24 The do's and don'ts of banning political extremism

> No one pretends that democracy is perfect or all-wise. Indeed it has been said that democracy is the worst form of Government except for all those other forms that have been tried from time to time.
>
> Winston Churchill[1]

One of the crucial questions within our liberal democracies is: how can a liberal democracy defend itself against extremist challengers without undermining its own core values? Unfortunately, academics and politicians seldom address this question, and few states have clear laws about it. The main exception is Germany, which responded to the Weimar trauma by creating a so-called *Wehrhafte Demokratie* or militant democracy. Simply stated, within a militant democracy there is no political space for extremists, i.e. anti-democrats. On the other extreme is the United States, which upholds the idea that democracy is a marketplace of ideas and functions best if all ideas are included. Consequently, the US has traditionally employed a very broad interpretation of freedom of speech, much broader than other western democracies, even though significant limitations have been introduced since 9/11, most notably with regard to speech supporting (Jihadist) terrorism. Most western democracies are closer to the German than the US model, even if they don't officially consider, let alone legally define, themselves as militant democracies.[2]

Every democracy is confronted with the question of how to defend itself at one time or another. If we limit ourselves to the postwar era, most western democracies have struggled with fascist groups directly after the Second World War, with communist organizations during the Cold War, with far right parties since the 1980s, and with Islamist groups since 9/11. Almost all states have responded on an ad hoc basis, without much fundamental reflection or public debate. Many of the attempts to ban 'anti-democratic' organizations were either irrelevant – i.e. banning groups with little to no political or social relevance, such as the National Democratic Party (NDP)

in Austria or the Center Party 86 (CP'86) in the Netherlands – or unsuc-
cessful – such as the attempted bans of the far left Communist Party of
Germany (KPD) in the 1950s and the far right German National Democratic
Party (NPD) at the beginning of the 21st century.

This year banning allegedly 'fascist' groups is back on the agenda in
several European countries. After recovering from the fiasco of 2001–2003,
when the case fell apart because the NPD was so deeply infiltrated by
intelligence services that the Constitutional Court could not distinguish
between party and state, Germany has started a second attempt to ban
the NPD. France is considering a ban of the Jewish Defence League (LDJ
in France; JDL in rest of world), an international Jewish nationalist-religious
organization founded in the United States in the 1960s by the late Rabbi
Meir Kahane. Finally, the most prominent case is the extreme right
political party Golden Dawn (XA) in Greece, which has attracted between
six and nine per cent of the national vote in recent elections. While all cases
are different, they all address exactly the same fundamental question: what
are the limits of political activism within a liberal democracy?

In the hope of generating a broader and more fundamental discussion
about the essential issue of militant democracy, I offer one do and two don'ts
of banning political extremism in general, and 'fascism' in particular. Before
I do, let me say a few words about my own view of liberal democracy.
Simply stated, liberal democracy is based on the ideas of popular sovereignty,
majority rule, rule of law, and minority protections. In line with the famous
adagio of Winston Churchill, I believe that liberal democracy is the least
bad form of government available today. This means that I support it, accept
that it has flaws, and believe that a better system could be developed in the
future. It also means that I think some ideas are better than others, but no
idea can lay claim to eternal truth. Finally, I believe that politics is often
conflictual in nature and creates winners and losers.

Now let's move on to the question of how to deal with political extremists.

Don't ban extremist speech!

The protection of the political rights of minorities is one of the key features
that sets *liberal* democracy apart from democracy per se. I limit myself here
to political minorities, i.e. groups that hold a minority political opinion, even
if the basis of that group and opinion is based on a specific identity (e.g.
ethnicity, gender, race, religion, sexuality, etc.). In contemporary western
democracies extremists are political minorities. I argue that extremists, like
all (political) minorities, should be allowed to voice their opinions uncon-
ditionally, even if their views are not shared by the majority, and therefore
not expressed in the state policies. There are several reasons for this.

First of all, I believe that democracy functions best when citizens have optimal information about the views of their fellow citizens. Hence, by having minority views expressed openly and unconstrained, the majority knows what the minority really thinks. They can then decide to take their views into account or to ignore them. Even the latter provides important information for the minority, who know that the majority ignores them rather than simply doesn't know what they want. If minorities cannot freely express their opinions, either they or some 'interpreter' will provide a limited or false opinion – think of the many political commentators reading the minds of the far right voter ('they are not really racist, but want to protest their social marginalization as a consequence of mass immigration'). In both cases the majority does not get accurate or full information and cannot adequately accommodate minority views even if they would want to.

Second, having extremist opinions out in the open forces democrats to justify their positions. The possible benefit of this is not, as is sometimes argued, that an open debate can change the minds of the extremists – at least not of the extremist elites. The main benefactor is the democratic majority. Being challenged politically, guards against complacency and tyranny of the majority and helps ensure that they do things for the right reasons. It also explains to people who might not instinctively support the policies, why they are supported, countering the false reasoning that extremists often provide. This can only strengthen trust in the democratic system.

The issue of immigration provides a perfect example of the democratic problems of a censored debate. For decades most western democracies significantly limited the public debate on immigration (and integration) by keeping it off the political agenda and, when that failed, extending anti-discrimination laws and increasing their enforcement. This lack of debate fuelled ignorance about both the facts of immigration and the motivations of immigration policy. It also led to the ignoring of some of the negative aspects of the developing 'multicultural society,' such as high crime and high unemployment of *certain* immigrant groups, which were then presented and explained in an ideological manner by the far right. By the time the democrats finally realized they had to respond in a non-repressive manner, they lacked both the convincing arguments and the legitimacy among many citizens.

Third, I strongly believe in the therapeutic value of free speech. For at least some citizens it is more important to voice their opinions than to have them implemented in policies. They can accept being overruled by the majority (only) as long as they have a right to express their opinion freely. After all, it is only after your argument has been included in the public debate that you can truly accept that it has not been able to convince the majority of your fellow citizens. Believe me, I know what I'm talking about, as I seem to hold a minority opinion on virtually all political issues (including this one).

Fourth, and related, by accepting their speech you give extremists a stake in the liberal democratic system. If extremists truly believe that they are the voice of the people, as the popular slogan of parties like the Flemish Interest (VB) and National Front (FN) goes, they will be willing to play by the democratic rules, i.e. free and fair elections, as long as everyone can contest the elections and express their views freely. This will also strengthen the 'moderate,' non-violent, factions vis-à-vis the 'extreme,' violent factions within larger extremist groups. The most striking example of this process is Northern Ireland, where the non-violent political party Sinn Féin (SF) eventually convinced the violent terrorist group Irish Republican Army (IRA) that their shared goal could be advanced more successfully *within* the British democratic system.

One of the arguments in favor of banning extremist speech is that the state otherwise condones it. For example, a Hungarian court ruled that it was the state's obligation to ban the far right paramilitary group Hungarian Guard because it would otherwise silently approve of it. But is the opposite from banning really approving? Democracies *tolerate* various behaviors and opinions that they don't necessarily *approve* of. That is the essence of tolerance, a basic value of liberal democracy. In fact, we generally refer to a political regime that bans everything it doesn't approve of as authoritarian rather than democratic.

But what if extremists say hurtful things about other groups, other minorities? Don't they have a right to be protected too? There is no doubt that extremists *do* say hurtful things about other groups, including minorities, but so do many majorities! The problem with 'hurt,' of course, is that it cannot be objectively measured. Who can prove that the statement that 'all immigrants are criminals' is more hurtful to an immigrant than the statement 'all FN voters are racists' is to a FN voter? Leaving aside that the level of hurt will differ significantly within the categories of 'immigrant' and 'FN voter.' In other words, political debate will always hurt some individuals and, because of the subjectivity of hurt, is impossible to legislate. Therefore, if there is to be any restriction on the political debate, it should be the same for any other debate, i.e. libel and slander – although I only reluctantly admit to these exceptions.

Finally, what about the argument that 'hate speech' can lead to the growth of prejudice among the majority population, thereby giving rise to extremist policies? Despite the popularity of this claim, there is very little empirical evidence of this actually playing out in contemporary western democracies. For example, it seems far more likely that the rise of far right parties were the *consequence* rather than the *cause* of widespread xenophobia within the population. Prejudice cannot be banned, only the open expression of it can, which might stop it from becoming official policy, but will not protect minorities from day-to-day confrontations with prejudice in less regulated social spaces. More importantly, the only way to truly overcome prejudice is by convincing people that prejudice is wrong to *hold*, not just to *express*. This can only be achieved by openly engaging these prejudices in political and public debates. If we believe that democrats cannot win this debate, as is often claimed in support of broad anti-discrimination laws, we do not really believe in democracy.

Don't ban democratic participation of extremist groups!

Some democracies are fairly tolerant toward individual extremist speech, but very restrictive on collective extremist political participation. They ban extremist organizations from regular political participation, such as the organization in political groups and parties, demonstrations in the streets, contesting elections, etc. The main reasons why I oppose this position have been laid out above; notably the argument that this denies extremists a stake in the democratic system and that it weakens the non-violent faction within the extremist camp. Also, it takes away the possibility for a better political system to emerge and develop. After all, liberal democracy is the best system we have . . . at this point.

They key question here, of course, is what do you do when the extremists come to power by democratic means? After all, as we hear over and over again, Adolf Hitler came to power through (by and large) free and fair elections! Truth is, however, that though Hitler did win some elections, he came to power because other non-democrats enabled him to form a government. Within Europe, no extremist party ever won a majority of the votes in free and fair elections. In fact, the case that comes closest, even though the elections were not really free and fair, is the 1991 Algerian legislative election, in which the Islamic Salvation Army (FIS) won 47.3 per cent of the vote in the first round. The military consequently canceled the second round, suspended democracy, and the country spiraled into a very bloody civil war.

There are two important lessons to be drawn from these two cases. First, extremists have only come to power through democratic elections in a few exceptional cases. The Weimar Republic was Germany's first attempt to build a democratic system with an exceptionally open and tolerant constitution. This was done in the aftermath of a devastating war and during an unprecedented economic crisis, while virtually all major political organizations were openly hostile to (liberal) democracy: from the communists to the Nazis and from the Catholics to the German nationalists. In the early

20th century only some ten countries in the world could be qualified as democratic, and then only if we overlook the fact that half of the citizenry (women) were excluded from the vote. Today democracy is hegemonic throughout the western world, with over 85 per cent of the population supporting democratic values in virtually every country. If the Nazis were only able to attract roughly one-third of the vote of the mostly non-democratic German people during the perfect storm of the Interwar period, we should have much less to fear from extremist parties today. Even more importantly, while Hitler was faced with opposition from other non-democrats, contemporary extremists are opposed by strongly democratic elites and masses.

The second lesson, based on the Algerian case, teaches us that you cannot save a democracy by excluding the majority of the population. After all, the essence of any democracy, liberal or otherwise, is popular sovereignty and majority rule. Once a majority of the people does not support democracy, the only options left are autocratic. This is not to say that the differences between the various autocratic options are irrelevant, for instance between Plato's philosopher king or Germany's genocidal Nazis. But the democratic option is no longer on the table. Obviously this also means that, should extremists ever come to power through free and fair elections in an established democracy, democrats are no longer beholden to regain power by democratic rules.

Do ban intrinsically violent extremist groups!

There is only one legitimate reason to ban political organizations and that is the use of violence. This is, in fact, an aspect that is mentioned in the discussions in all three countries that are currently investigating the possibility of a ban. The German NPD ban was rejuvenated by the discovery of the National Socialist Underground, a neo-Nazi terrorist organization, and the dismal handling of its terrorism by the German state. While the link between the NPD and violence is relatively tenuous, it is clearer in the French case. LDJ members have been involved in several violent actions and in July 2014 two members were imprisoned for placing a bomb under the car of an anti-Zionist journalist in 2012. In the case of Golden Dawn the link is the strongest, as state investigators allege that the party actually consists of two separate structures: one open and essentially aimed at contesting elections and one hidden and involved in a violent campaign against political opponents.

To ban an extremist group the violence should be *intrinsic* to the group. In other words, the character of the group has to change fundamentally once the element of violence is removed. This is very often not the case with extremist groups. For example, the Dutch CP'86 was banned (in part) because of its link to violence, even though it had been low level and sporadic, and mainly linked to individual members, not the leadership, let alone the organization as such. The same seems to be true for the NPD. The LDJ could be a less clear-cut case, given the violent history of JDL groups in other parts of the world (notably Israel and the US), as well as the more sustained campaigns involving violence of the LDJ itself. That said, there seems to be no proof that violence is intrinsic to the organization. For example, many violent incidents are related to non-violent demonstrations, as a consequence of interactions with (violent) counter-demonstrators or with the police.

The only group that seems to fit this criterion well is Golden Dawn in Greece. While here much violence is also linked to specific activities and members, there is more. This is what a senior party member stated in an interview with the Greek newspaper *To Vima* on 24 September 2013:

> At Golden Dawn we have a full military structure with at least 3,000 people ready for everything! We have about 50 phalanxes for street fights and about as many 6-man commando strike forces for organized attacks, under the guidance of three organization members. The strike forces handle special attacks against immigrants or reprisals against enemies of the organization. Whatever that might mean.

If this turns out to be true, Golden Dawn is both a political party and a terrorist paramilitary unit *in one*. This means that violence is indeed intrinsic to Golden Dawn as an organization, and it should therefore be banned. At the same time, if a new party (e.g. National Dawn) would be founded that is an exact copy of Golden Dawn, i.e. openly anti-democratic and only slightly-veiled neo-Nazi, but without the terrorist paramilitary unit, it should be allowed to exist and contest elections.

A slightly more problematic situation exists in Hungary, where the Movement for a Better Hungary (Jobbik), a political party, is closely linked to the now banned Hungarian Guard, an unarmed paramilitary organization responsible for intimidation and violence, most notably against the Roma minority in the East of the country. While the connections between the two are extremely close – for example, Jobbik party leader Gabor Vona was a co-founder of the Hungarian Guard – these are legally two separate political organizations. Consequently, even if the Hungarian state would conclude that violence is intrinsic to the Hungarian Guard, this would not automatically mean that the same conclusion can be drawn for Jobbik, as some have suggested.

In short, a key feature of liberal democracy is that it tolerates, not necessarily approves, its political opponents. It is based on the rule of the people, which presupposes a trust in at least the majority of those people. This again means a trust in their ability to choose, in majority, the democratic options in free and fair elections. Letting everyone speak and organize, including extremists, strengthens liberal democracy by giving everyone both a voice and a stake in the system. It guards against complacency and tyranny of the majority and keeps the possibility open that an even better system could emerge. The only price we should ask of everyone, extremists *and* democrats alike, is that they play by the democratic rules, i.e. realizing your political ambitions exclusively by non-violent means.

Notes

1   Richard Langworth (ed.), *Churchill by Himself: The Definitive Collection of Quotations*. New York: PublicAffairs, 2008, p. 574.
2   For an overview of the situation in several countries, see Markus Thiel (ed.), *The 'Militant Democracy' Principle in Modern Democracies*. Farnham, UK: Ashgate, 2009. For an original philosophical defence, see Alexander S. Kirschner, *A Theory of Militant Democracy: The Ethics of Combatting Political Extremism*. New Haven, CT: Yale University Press, 2014.

25 No, we are not all Charlie (and that's a problem)

The tragic terrorist attack on the French satirist magazine *Charlie Hebdo* in Paris, killing ten journalists and two policemen, is frightening at many levels. Although the three terrorists are still at large, and the official motivation hasn't been established yet, all indications point to Jihadists, probably French-born Muslims who returned from the war in Syria[1] – note the similarities with the terrorist attack at the Jewish Museum in Brussels in May 2014.

The general response has been one that we have seen too often before, for example after the killing of Dutch filmmaker Theo van Gogh in 2004 or the terrorist attacks in the US of 2011. Politicians use the attacks to boast about the perfect democratic and free society that they preside over and stress that this has nothing to do with Islam, but with some pathological individuals who use a religion as an excuse for extremist ideas. Citizens respond in the one medium in which they are still active, social media, and make grand statements of solidarity, before being distracted by a video of a waterskiing squirrel or a piano-playing kitten. Both will declare that we are all whomever the victim of the day is.

Today Facebook and Twitter are full of statements like 'Je suis Charlie' (I am Charlie) and 'we are all Charlie.' Unfortunately, we are not. Or, more precisely, with very few exceptions, we are not Charlie, and that is a major problem for liberal democracies around the world. Let me give you three reasons why most of us are not Charlie and why this is problematic for our democracies.

First, many of the most vocal defenders of *Charlie Hebdo* are very new and selective fans of the satirist magazine. For instance, it is amazing how many Islamophobic and far right people are declaring their love for a magazine that until recently they would criticize as a 'communist rag' – as Charlie's biting satire also mocked their own heroes, from Jesus Christ to Marine Le Pen. These are the heroic defenders of free speech, like Geert Wilders, who want to ban the Quran because it incites violence.

Many people are not Charlie exactly because *Charlie Hebdo* would criticize *all* religions and *all* politicians, irrespective of their ethnicity, gender, ideology, etcetera. Consequently, leaders of all religions and political parties have criticized them. That said, they have only been violently attacked by extremist Muslims. This is a fact that can and should not be denied! This is not to say that *only* Muslim extremists attack their critics – for example, recently two French members of the Jewish Defence League (LDJ) were convicted for placing a bomb under the car of an anti-Zionist journalist. Still, this does not take away from the *fact* that many (and probably most) acts and threats of political violence in contemporary Europe come from extremist Muslims. This is not *because of* Islam, as 99.9 per cent of Muslims are not violent, but it also doesn't mean that Islam plays *no* role at all.

Second, many people are not Charlie because they believe that democratic debates should be 'civil' and not upset people. The problem is that 'civility' is a slippery concept, which means very different things to different people. Similarly, it is impossible to measure whether people are upset, let alone objectively compare how upset they are. People can get upset about everything, so why should religious sensitivity have special protection (see also Chapter 24). Who is to say that Charlie's critique of Islam(ism) upsets a very religious Muslim more than *l'Equipe*'s critique of Paris Saint Germain hurts a diehard PSG fan?

Throughout history civility has been defined in line with the interests of the political establishment. This is still the case, which means that the civility argument is almost always used selectively and opportunistically. Certain groups are protected from 'uncivil' discourse and others are not – as is the case with anti-discrimination legislation. This shields these groups from criticism, irrespective of the accuracy of the critique, which in the long term hurts not just the critics but also the (not) criticized, who have no incentives to reflect and improve.

Third, and final, many people are not Charlie because they are afraid. They never openly criticize anything or anyone, or at least not relatively powerful people. But even among professional critics, such as comedians and intellectuals, self-censorship is increasingly becoming the norm. Many treat issues related to Jews and Israel much more sensitively than other groups and states, out of fear of professional sanctions – think about the recent Salaita case in the United States. Similarly troubling is the growing group of comedians and intellectuals self-censoring themselves on topics related to Islam and Muslims. Already several years ago I met Dutch public intellectuals who told me, in confidence, that they had stopped criticizing Islam(ism) in public because of violent threats to them and their family. Even the 'fearless' US comedian Stephen Colbert would not show the (in)famous Mohammed cartoons, or other images deemed offensive to Muslims, instead putting up a (funny) image of 'technical disturbances.' While making fun of his fear of a violent response, he never seriously problematized it, and, in the end, censored himself. Even the few brave souls that do dare to satirize Islam(ism), often get censored by the media or their employers – South Park's notorious Mohammed episode has been censored multiple times by Comedy Central!

To be sure, there are structural explanations for the high levels of anger and frustration of part of the (radical) Muslim population in Europe as well as for the fact that *some* among them resort to (the threat of) violence. None of these *excuse* violent actions within democracies, but that doesn't mean that we cannot learn from them. It is comforting and politically expedient to claim that 'we' are attacked because 'they' cannot deal with 'our' freedoms, particularly freedom of speech. Politicians will preach that 'Muslims' have to come to terms with the fact that 'they' (now) live in a society where everything can be criticized, pointing to critiques and satires about Christians and Christianity (often of the 1960s and 1970s though), but this is at best naive and at worst disingenuous. Many 'acceptable' critiques of Islam and Muslims would be deemed unacceptable, and illegal (!), if they targeted other groups – as a test, just replace 'Muslims' for 'Jews' or 'blacks' and see whether you still think the critique is acceptable. Hence, certain Muslims will see the 'freedom of speech' argument as a cop-out.

Related to this is the perception of powerlessness among the Muslim populations of Europe. Some feel that Muslims are discriminated against because they don't have a voice in the political system. They at times point the finger at the power of Jews, admittedly *sometimes* inspired by an anti-Semitic worldview, and their successful attempt to more effectively suppress anti-Semitism. They feel that Muslims have either to rely on the sympathy of non-Muslim elites, who turn out to be fairly selective in their support (even on the left), or resort to extra-political measures, such as (the threat of) violence.

Let me repeat that these are *not* acceptable excuses for violent actions or speech! But they are also not without a factual base. If 'we' are going to expect of 'them' to abide by 'our' freedom of speech, than this freedom of speech should either be totally free or protect all groups equally (which, I believe, is impossible). If 'we' want 'them' to abide by *the* (not 'our') democratic rules of the game, 'we' should also accept 'them' as equal citizens. Too often Islam and Muslims are treated as foreign, either linked to immigration or to a foreign country/region. But the majority of Muslims in most European countries are citizens, born and raised in Europe. In other words, 'they' are part of 'we'! So, as much as 'they' have to come to terms with living in 'our' country, 'we' have to come to terms with the fact that it is 'their' country too!

So, how do we move forward in a constructive manner, strengthening our liberal democracies rather than weakening them by authoritarian kneejerk reactions. Rather than narrowing freedom of speech further, by limiting it to 'civil' speech or by broadening anti-discrimination legislation even more, we should live up to our slogans and truly embrace freedom of speech for *all*, including anti-Semites and Islamophobes! Similarly, we should criticize and satirize *all*, from atheists to Christians, from Jews to Muslims, and from Greens to the far right. This requires not only that we all speak out against extremists, but also that we defend those who take them on . . . even *before* they get threatened or killed.

Note

1   The terrorists were two brothers, born in France to Algerian immigrants, who had both been involved in supporting Jihadist groups in the Middle East. One of the brothers had trained with al Qaeda in Yemen. Both brothers were killed in a shoot-out with security forces a few days later.

26 What freedom of speech?

Of foxes, chickens and #jesuischarlie

> We reaffirm our unfailing attachment to the freedom of expression, to human rights, to pluralism, to democracy, to tolerance and to the rule of law: They are the foundation of our democracies and are at the heart of the European Union. By attacking Charlie Hebdo, police officers and the Jewish community, the terrorists set out to tear down these universal values. They will not succeed.
>
> Joint Statement of EU Ministers of Interior,
> 11 January 2015

There is a Dutch saying, which literally translates as 'When the fox preaches passion, farmer look after your chickens.' Call me paranoid, or perhaps cautious, but this is a motto I tend to abide by when following politics. In fact, experience teaches us that the more passionate the fox(es), the better one should look after the chickens. Unfortunately, few of us do. We get mesmerized by the passion of the fox and don't see how our chickens disappear, one by one. Enter #JeSuisCharlie!

On the day of the horrific terrorist attack on the French satirical magazine *Charlie Hebdo*, I published a piece entitled 'No, we are NOT all Charlie (and that's a problem)' (see Chapter 25), which went viral.[1] No one knows why, least of all me, but it clearly hit a nerve. I argued that we (and I include myself) are not Charlie, because of at least one of the following three reasons: (1) we are selective defenders of free speech; (2) we believe that speech should be 'civil'; and, the one that also applies to me, (3) we are afraid to stand up to people who threaten violence in response to contested speech.

While #JeSuisCharlie might not have been the most popular hashtag in history, it was already used more than 5 million times within the first two days after the attack. Absolutely everyone was Charlie, from embattled Muslims and their far right enemies in France to authoritarian dictators in Africa and hip coffee shop owners in Santiago de Chile. Millions of people demonstrated in defence of democracy and free speech around the world.

In Paris some 1.6 million marched through the streets on 11 January, one of the largest rallies in postwar France. As many critics noted, the rally included noted defenders of democracy and free speech, such as Malian President Ibrahim Boubacar Keita and Jordan's King Abdullah II.

As so often happens in the aftermath of a traumatic 'attack on democracy,' a short burst of emotional support for democracy is followed by a calculated, less visible, attack on its core values. Just as 9/11 was the start of the most significant assault on liberal democracy in recent US history, the terrorist attacks in Paris have given rise to a broad onslaught on the core values of liberal democracy in Europe, not least that of freedom of speech.

It started out with a still fairly benign condemnation of the few people who did not get swallowed up by the #JeSuisCharlie hype and a more vocal rejection of those who dared to present a different narrative. Perhaps the first high-profile case of JeSuisCharlie-hypocrisy was the arrest of the controversial French comedian and anti-Zionist Dieudonné M'bala M'bala, who, after allegedly having marched in the big Paris demonstration, posted on his Facebook page, 'As far as I am concerned, I feel I am Charlie Coulibaly' – referring to the terrorist attacker of the Paris kosher deli two days after the Charlie Hebdo attack. While he was quickly released, few came to his defence. We were Charlie, not Dieudonné!

Within days the civility argument resurfaced with a vengeance. While those who dared to claim that the cartoonists had called the violence upon themselves were (rightly) condemned, the argument that their cartoons were 'racist' and not satirical – as if the two are mutually exclusive – steadily gained ground. On the left and the right of the political spectrum people returned to their previous positions, arguing even more vigilantly against the specific speech they didn't like – while often either claiming to be Charlie or defending the speech they did like with references to freedom of speech.

One of the most bizarre debates was in Belgium, where almost the whole cultural and political elite tumbled over each other to reject the 'unacceptable' banner of Standard Liège ultras – which featured the horror movie persona Jason Voorhees holding the (beheaded) head of former Standard captain Steven Defour, now playing for opponent, and archrival, RSC Anderlecht. In all these cases politicians argued that, while they fully supported #JeSuisCharlie and free speech, this particular speech 'crossed the line' and was 'unacceptable.' In most cases the silence of the earlier defenders of freedom of speech was deafening.

Of much greater consequence, however, is the myriad of new legislations that is being prepared and proposed across Europe. Barely back home from their demonstration for free speech in Paris, political leaders from across the European Union (EU) started discussing new limitations on free speech to 'fight radicalism.'

Once again the proposed policies to protect liberal democracy meant the weakening of key aspects of liberal democracy. In one of the most significant statements, interior ministers of eleven EU member states (including Germany, Poland, Spain and the UK) used the attacks to call for (even) further collaboration between their law enforcement and intelligence agencies. In a perfect example of newspeak, they stated:

> We are concerned at the increasingly frequent use of the Internet to fuel hatred and violence and signal our determination to ensure that the Internet is not abused to this end, while safeguarding that it remains, in scrupulous observance of fundamental freedoms, a forum for free expression, in full respect of the law.

The uncomfortable truth is, however, that Europe has always had an *un*scrupulous observance of fundamental freedoms. While openly preaching freedom of speech European governments have always limited this freedom for specific groups (e.g. communist and fascists) and with regard to specific topics (e.g. monarchy and religion).

These limitations became even more numerous in the 1980s, as a consequence of a true explosion of new 'anti-discrimination' legislation. The new legislation, as well as the accompanying centres to 'fight' discrimination, barely distinguish between 'discriminatory' behaviours and opinions, outlawing a broad range of speech.

Since 9/11 the focus has changed again, as many European states have become much less concerned about Islamophobic speech – which is now the most protected 'hate speech' in Europe – and much more about Jihadist speech. Almost after each 'Jihadist' attack, governments across the continent develop new infringements on rights to privacy and free speech. For example, since the Charlie Hebdo attacks the French government has aggressively reigned in vocal support for terrorism. The new limitations come on top of a long-established line of limitations. The *New York Times* (15 January 2015) reported that up to 100 people are currently under investigation in France 'for making or posting comments that support or try to justify terrorism.'

Sadly enough, this selective defence of free speech seems to be more in line with Charlie than I initially realized. While most mainstream media continue to portray *Charlie Hebdo* as a pure and principled satirical magazine that targeted everyone and everything, it turns out that Charlie made exceptions too. In 1996 three prominent cartoonists of *Charlie Hebdo*, including the late Stéphane Charbonnier (Charb), collected almost 175,000 signatures in a petition to ban the far right party *National Front* (FN), because it allegedly contradicted the key values of the French Republic. Even more damaging, the magazine fired cartoonist Maurice Sinet (Siné) for an allegedly anti-Semitic cartoon in 2008. Sinet successfully sued *Charlie Hebdo* for 40,000 euros for wrongful termination in 2009.

In short, freedom of speech has always been limited and selective in Europe. Unfortunately, this is completely in line with the preferences of the vast majority of Europeans, even though they quarrel over which specific speech should be free and which should be banned.

The main problem is that most Europeans, both at the elite and mass level, have a grossly inflated idea of the extent of freedom of speech in Europe, a direct consequence of the uncritical and self-congratulatory discourse on the topic. Hence, they argue that speech was never meant to be totally free (e.g. Pope Francis) and that 'some' limitations are perfectly democratic. The problem is that we already have *many* limitations of free speech in Europe. The constant adding of more 'exceptions' has created a situation in which it has become simply inaccurate and disingenuous to claim that Europe has (true) freedom of speech.

Note

1   Within a month it was viewed more than 200,000 times on the *Open Democracy* website and was shared more than 20,000 times on Facebook. It was also translated and re-published in a broad variety of newspapers, including *Ara* (Spain), *De Morgen* (Belgium), *Die Tageszeitung* (Germany), *Information* (Denmark), *NRC Handelsblad* (Netherlands), and *Svenska Dagbladet* (Sweden).

27   As Europe looks fearfully outside, its liberal democracy is under attack from within

Far right parties are at record highs in opinion polls and are winning in local and national elections, as refugee centres burn and tens of thousands demonstrate against an alleged 'Muslim invasion.' If one is to believe the international media the 'refugee crisis' is pushing Europe into the hands of the far right. In October 2015 the Swiss People's Party (SVP) won 29.4 per cent of the vote in the Swiss national elections, the largest victory of any far right party in Western Europe since 1945. In the Netherlands and Sweden, long seen as immune to far right parties (see Chapter 21), the Party for Freedom (PVV) and Sweden Democrats (SD) are soaring in the polls. And from Denmark to Germany (planned) refugee centres are targeted by arsonists and protesters.

Against this angry mob, given voice by charismatic leaders like Marine Le Pen and Heinz-Christian Strache, stands an apathetic and flustered political elite. While German Chancellor Angela Merkel tried to defend a welcoming approach to the refugees, she met with silence or opposition from her centre-left and centre-right colleagues across the continent. In the Netherlands, premier Mark Rutte decided to hide in the US, supporting the Dutch business community at visits to Atlanta and Washington, leaving the political debate on refugees to PVV leader Geert Wilders. In France and the United Kingdom, political leaders responded hesitantly, coming across as incompetent and wavering compared to their decisive and vocal far right competitors. As Merkel slowly changed her welcoming discourse – under huge pressure from her Bavarian partner, the powerful Christian Social Union (CSU), and her own youth branch, the Young Union (JU) – politicians across the European Union (EU) started to express more boldly their opposition toward refugees and promote stricter border controls.

All of this is disheartening for anyone concerned with liberal democracy in Europe, but it is not new. In the 1990s even larger groups of citizens protested refugee centres in the recently reunited Germany and deadly attacks on refugees and other minorities were a common occurrence. Similarly, far right parties gained significant results in countries like Austria and France, while mainstream parties tightened immigration and hardened their discourse. What *is* new, but unfortunately mostly ignored, is that for the first time in postwar history liberal democracy in Europe is attacked from within the political elite, rather than only from outside of it.

As commentators continue to be blinded by the usual suspects such as Marine Le Pen and their (alleged) influence on opportunistic mainstream politicians like Nicolas Sarkozy, they fail to see that the real damage is being done by sitting premiers and presidents, most notably in East Central Europe. For whatever the problems involved in the 'far right light' policies of politicians like Rutte and Sarkozy, they never intended to build a different Europe. In fact, these politicians claimed that these right-wing measures are necessary to strengthen liberal democracy in Europe and to ensure its survival in light of far right and other challenges.

Enter Viktor Orbán, prime minister of Hungary, and liberal-turned-conservative-turned-far right politician (see also Chapter 7). Since regaining power in 2010, Orbán has consistently undermined the liberal safeguards of Hungarian democracy, most notably through introducing a new constitution and making a host of political appointments in old and new state institutions. He openly declared that liberal democracy has no future and that he wants to transform Hungary into an illiberal democracy. As long as the EU didn't interfere in his domestic power grab, and it hardly did, Orbán did not really try to influence broader European politics. But this year things changed. In January 2015 he used the terrorist attack on *Charlie Hebdo* (see Chapter 25) to start his own attack on multiculturalism. Not just in Hungary, but also in Europe as a whole. As other world leaders marched for free speech and tolerance, Orbán called upon the EU to restrict access to migrants with 'different cultural characteristics.'

Even before the 'refugee crisis' hit Europe this summer, Orbán had already initiated a bogus 'referendum' on immigration, in which immigrants were directly linked to terrorism and unemployment. Once Hungary became a major destination for Syrian (and other) refugees, his government did the utmost to create the impression that they were a threat to national order and security. More importantly he went on a direct attack against the 'old' European model, exemplified by Merkel, propagating his alternative. In his own 'rivers of blood' speech, Orbán stated:

> What we have at stake today is Europe, the European way of life, the survival or disappearance of European values and nations, or their transformation beyond recognition . . . We would like Europe to be preserved for the Europeans. But there is something we would not just like but we want because it only depends on us: we want to preserve a Hungarian Hungary.

Not meeting any serious pushback, Orbán took his 'new' politics to the heart of Europe's 'old' politics, the European People's Party (EPP) Congress in Madrid. On the home turf of Merkel, he argued in typical far right fashion that 'immigrants' (he doesn't recognize them as refugees) are a threat, referring to them as 'an army,' helped by the left-wing parties, who will destroy Europe.

While most centre-right politicians in Western Europe don't openly embrace Orbán's vision of a 'Christian Europe' of strong nation states, with perhaps the exception of the influential CSU, several more and less openly herald him as the guardian of Europe's borders and support his call for stricter border control. In East Central Europe support is much more open. Both Czech president Miloš Zeman and Slovak premier Robert Fico have gone on Islamophobic rants of their own, while current and former leaders in other countries have embraced Orbán's far right vision of Europe. The Polish government kept its distance, but will be replaced by the right-wing populist Law and Justice (PiS) party soon, whose leader Jarosław Kaczyński has been praising Orbán's 'Budapest Model' since 2011.

With a growing group of closet far right leaders and their tacit supporters in the governments of EU member states, challenging the status quo of liberal democratic Europe, it is high time that the true liberal democratic parties and politicians respond. Socialists & Democrats (S&D), the social democratic group in the European Parliament (EP), has taken a first step, putting the expulsion of Fico and his Smer party on the agenda. In sharp contrast, the EPP, the most powerful political group in the EU, has consistently protected Orbán against EU sanctions and even applauded his classic far right speech at the Madrid Congress. While some opposition is finally starting to be voiced within the EPP, few prominent members are calling for the expulsion of Orbán and his Fidesz party. EPP president Joseph Daul, who is a long-time and vocal supporter of Orbán, hides behind the argument that the EPP would lose its influence over them if they would expel Fidesz. What that influence exactly is, he has never said.

After years of crying wolf, it might no longer be easy to convince the increasing skeptical European citizenry that liberal democracy in Europe is truly in danger. They have heard it before, many times since the late 1980s, after every modest election success of a far right party. But this time it is different. This time the threat comes from within the European elite and goes to the core of the European power structure. And it is gaining ground fast, with Poland the newest ally. If the European leadership in general, and the EPP in particular, doesn't change its short-sighted opportunistic strategy and finally stand up for its core values, that much feared future election victory of Marine Le Pen in France might not even matter that much anymore.

Epilogue
European democracy after Paris

I felt really good, that Friday afternoon, as I had finally finished the full manuscript of this book, sent it off to the publisher, and was ready to start a well-deserved weekend away from dark thoughts about the dwindling state of liberal democracy in Europe. Not being the superstitious type, I hadn't even realized it was Friday the 13th, and even if I had known, I would have laughed it off and looked for a ladder to walk under. When I came home, I saw a text message from a colleague: 'Did you see the attack at the soccer match in France?!!!'

He was, of course, referring to what has since become known as the 'Paris Attacks' of 13 November, which killed a total of 130 people and injured 368. This orgy of mass shootings and suicide bombings was undoubtedly the worst terrorist attack in Europe this century, not because of the number of people killed – which was higher in the Madrid train bombings of 2004 (191) – but because of the required coordination and the scope of the attacks. The terrorists had attacked the key recreational sites of city life – related to food, music, and sports – and had done so at the same time! That it had been done in Paris, the city that had suffered the *Charlie Hebdo* attack at the beginning of the year (see Chapter 25), made it even more unsettling. After all, of all European cities, Paris must have been at the highest level of security.

I spent that evening and weekend in a haze, shocked by the atrocities in Paris, annoyed by the social media posts about the selective sympathy (which was upsetting their selective sympathy), but mostly worried about the inevitable overreaction by France and other European Union (EU) member states. I had never believed that there was a fundamental ideological difference between the EU states that opposed the Iraq invasion and those and the US that supported it. Countries like Belgium and France just had made a different strategic calculation and had hidden that under a more popular liberal democratic veneer. As I hoped that France would follow Norway after Breivik rather than the US after 9/11 (see Chapter 23), I knew they would have the same knee-jerk response as the Americans, egged on by hysterical masses and opportunistic elites. Still, I hadn't expected it to be this bad.

Within hours the European elite shot into war-mongering mode. President François Holland, embattled by an image of weak leadership and a resurgent far right, transformed into a French George W. Bush, vowing a 'merciless' fight against terrorism in which he would 'wipe out' the 'army of fanatics' behind the attack, i.e. the Islamic State (ISIS). The frenzy spread across the continent. British Prime Minister David Cameron told Hollande that 'your fight is our fight,' while Dutch premier Mark Rutte, who had explicitly rejected the idea of a 'war' on terrorism after the *Charlie Hebdo* attack of January, now declared resolutely that the Netherlands was 'at war with ISIS.'

Several leading politicians used the opportunity to push through their anti-immigration agenda by linking the terrorists to the refugee crisis. Well before there was any evidence for a link between the terrorists and the refugees, which even two weeks later is still dubious at best, leading politicians of the Bavarian Christian Social Union (CSU) and the Polish Law and Justice (PiS) argued that 'Paris changes everything' and 'the time of uncontrolled immigration' has to come to an end. In the United States a majority of governors declared their state closed to Syrian refugees and all presidential candidates for the Republican Party called upon President Obama not to accept (non-Christian) Syrian refugees any longer. Predictably, Hungarian Prime Minister Viktor Orbán took it even a step further, stating: 'Of course it's not accepted, but the factual point is that all the terrorists are basically migrants. The question is *when* they migrated to the European Union' (see also Chapters 7 and 27).

In a direct response to the attacks Hollande declared a state of emergency in France, as military and police established a massive presence in the streets of Paris and security forces started rounding up 'suspects' across the country. When it was established that several of the terrorists had operated from Molenbeek, a Brussels district known for its large number of North African immigrants and their descendants, the 'war on terror' moved north, to the capital of Belgium and the EU. The Belgian government put Brussels under a lockdown, as policemen and soldiers patrolled the streets and seemingly randomly arrested young Muslim men – given that all but one were already released the next day. The threat level in Brussels was lowered after several days, from the highest four ('serious and imminent threat') to the second-highest three ('serious threat), while the French parliament voted to extend the state of emergency for three more months.

Obviously, it makes sense that terrorist attacks are followed by an immediate raising of the threat level and activity of security forces. The problem is that the 'emergency' measures are often extended for a significantly longer period and that there is little political or public debate and oversight over the effectiveness of these measures. Political leaders will scare the people and press them into submission with terrifying apocalyptic scenarios. For instance, French premier Manuel Valls warned that 'chemical or biological weapons' might be used on French soil and that 'no possibility can be excluded.' As so often, no evidence, beyond the self-serving 'indications' on the basis of secret intelligence, was provided for this outlandish claim. In Belgium the media for once came together across linguistic divides, following requests from the state to (self-)censor information about the security operations so as to not help the terrorists. In a painful expression of solidarity, citizens decided to post cat memes on social media, rather than criticize the media's decision or critically follow the state operations.

With the exception of a few targeted arrests in the first week, including a raid in a suburb of Paris in which one of the suspects blew himself up, the hundreds of security operations across Europe have mainly harassed people already under suspicion, in a feeble attempt to show the people that the state is in control of the situation. Almost all arrested people were released within days, despite the powers of the state of emergency in Brussels and France, and are left wondering whether there is any other feasible reason than their ethnicity and faith that they were single out. And as happened after the introduction of the PATRIOT ACT in the US, the French state has started to use its emergency powers to arrest, curtail, and harass people completely unconnected to the Paris attacks, such as environmental activists in the run-up to the great Climate Change Summit (COP21) in Paris.

The aftermath of the Paris attacks are a reminder of how easily people are scared into accepting 'emergency' measures and how easily these measures migrate from the original group to new, very different, groups. We know from responses to earlier attacks, most notably 9/11, that the emergency measures are never really temporary. While the worst infractions upon liberal democracy are later amended, but often only after significant legal and political pressure, the state never returns to exactly the same situation as before the terrorist attacks. Each attack weakens liberal democracy, and the real, long-term damage is not done by the terrorists, but by the counter-terrorists. It is from within the political and state elites that authoritarian measures are pushed through, under the cloak of fear and outrage, even if many of the measures are unrelated to the attacks – think about the Real ID Act that followed the 9/11 attacks, despite the fact that the attackers had a multitude of (fake) passports, or for the closing of the EU borders, even though almost all identified terrorists were EU born and raised.

There are many reasons why Europe's citizens accept these infringements upon their own rights. Many people believe that they won't affect them, as they are not Muslims or non-white (or whomever else is the identified target). The fact that these laws are always applied much more broadly once they are on the books, including to white middle class people (such as most of the environmentalists), should make them rethink this short-sighted, self-centred approach. Confusion and fear of the public are even more important. For some these wear off quickly, but often the damage is then already done. Moreover, as soon as the next terrorist attack or threat appears, and is hyped in the media, they will again happily accept the 'emergency' measures, desperate for state competency and societal security. The problem is that neither truly exists, at least not in a complete and unproblematic form.

The two major lies that feed the counter-terrorism policies that significantly weaken liberal democracy, are that states can be 100 per cent competent and societies can be 100 per cent safe. As we know from decades of state repression, even the most democratic states make (many) mistakes, ranging from the arrests and convictions of innocent people to rogue state programs like COINTELPRO in the US. At the same time, no society, not even within a dictatorship, is ever completely safe from terrorism. Ironically, while the costs of counter-terrorism programs are relatively clear, even though media and politicians mostly ignore them, the benefits are murky at best. In most cases the goals of the programs are so vague that it is impossible to objectively evaluate them. When is the 'war on terror' won? Is the PATRIOT ACT successful because there has been no new 9/11? And even when the goals would be clear, security protocol prevents an objective evaluation of the claimed successes – you know, the 'prevented terror attacks' that make the news whenever budgets or laws need to be renewed.

Within the liberal democratic paradigm the state is not considered inherently bad or good. Rather, it holds that a democratic state can function well if, and *only* if, its citizens limit the powers of the state and keep a check on its leaders. Ironically, as political distrust and dissatisfaction are at all-time highs in many European democracies, the vast majority of people are willing to give unprecedented powers to the leaders and states they don't like and trust. All because they buy into the illusion of a competent state than can ensure full security. To save liberal democracy from slowly but steadily destroying itself from within, we have to let go of this dangerous illusion, however uncomfortable it may be. Only if we accept the *reality* that no (democratic) state is completely competent and safe, are we able to protect our liberal democracy from both the terrorists and counter-terrorists.

Further reading

This is a very concise list of articles and books that provide more detailed and general discussions of the four themes addressed in this book. Almost all sources are academic, recent, and in English, and should be accessible to the readers of this book.

Far right

Akkerman, Tjitske, Sarah L. de Lange and Matthijs Rooduijn (eds), *Radical Right-Wing Populist Parties in Western Europe*. London: Routledge, 2016.

Langenbacher, Nora and Britta Schellenberg (eds), *Is Europe on the 'Right' Path? Right-Wing Extremism and Right-Wing Populism in Europe*. Berlin: Friedrich Ebert Stiftung, 2011, free download at http://library.fes.de/pdf-files/do/08338.pdf.

Minkenberg, Michael (ed.), *The Radical Right in Europe: An Overview*. Gütersloh: Verlag Bertelsmann Stiftung, 2008.

Minkenberg, Michael (ed.), *Transforming the Transformation? The East European Radical Right in the Political Process*. London: Routledge, 2016.

Mudde, Cas, *Populist Radical Right Parties in Europe*. Cambridge: Cambridge University Press, 2007

Mudde, Cas (ed.), *The Populist Radical Right: A Reader*. London: Routledge, 2016.

Populism

Canovan, Margaret, 'Trust the People! Populism and the Two Faces of Democracy. *Political Studies*, Vol. 47, No. 1, 1999, pp. 2–16.

Kriesi, Hanspeter and Takis Pappas (eds), *European Populism in the Shadow of the Great Recession*. Colchester, UK: ECPR Press, 2015.

Mudde, Cas, 'The Populist Zeitgeist', *Government and Opposition*, Vol. 39, No. 3, 2004, pp. 541–63.

Mudde, Cas and Cristóbal Rovira Kaltwasser (eds.), *Populism in Europe and the Americas: Threat or Corrective for Democracy?* Cambridge: Cambridge University Press, 2012.

Mudde, Cas and Cristóbal Rovira Kaltwasser, *Populism: A Very Short Introduction* Oxford: Oxford University Press, 2016.

Panizza, Francisco, *Populism and the Mirror of Democracy*. London: Verso, 2005.
Taggart, Paul, *Populism*. Buckingham, UK: Open University Press, 2000.

Euroscepticism

Kopecký, Petr and Cas Mudde, 'The Two Sides of Euroscepticism. Party Positions on European Integration in East Central Europe', *European Union Politics*, Vol. 3, No. 3, 2002, pp. 297–326.
Lefonte, Cécile, *Understanding Euroscepticism*. Basingstoke, UK: Palgrave Macmillan, 2010.
Pinder, John and Simon Usherwood, *The European Union: A Very Short Introduction*. Oxford: Oxford University Press, 2013, 3rd edn.
Szczerbiak, Aleks and Paul Taggart (eds), *Opposing Europe? The Comparative Party Politics of Euroscepticism*. Oxford: Oxford University Press, 2008, 2 volumes.
Taggart, Paul, 'A Touchstone of Dissent: Euroscepticism in Contemporary West European Party Systems', *European Journal of Political Research*, Vol. 33, 1998, pp. 363–88.
Usherwood, Simon and Nick Startin, 'Euroscepticism as a Persistent Phenomenon', *Journal of Common Market Studies*, Vol. 51, No. 1, 2013, pp. 1–16.

Liberal Democracy

Crick, Bernard, *Democracy: A Very Short Introduction*. Oxford: Oxford University Press, 2003.
Crouch, Colin, *Post-Democracy*. Oxford: Polity, 2004.
Kirschner, Alexander S., *A Theory of Militant Democracy: The Ethics of Combatting Political Extremism*. New Haven, CT: Yale University Press, 2014.
Mair, Peter, *Ruling the Void: The Hollowing of Western Democracy*. London: Verso, 2013.
Mudde, Cas, 'Liberal Democracies and the Extremist Challenge of the Early 21st Century', *Nordic Journal of Human Rights*, Vol. 21, No. 4, 2003, pp. 429–40.

Index

Hope not Hate 30
Hofstadter, Richard 4, 57
Hollande, Fran ois 150
Howard, John 48
Hungarian Democratic Forum (MDF)
47
Hungarian Guard 20, 132, 135,
Hungarian Justice and Life Party
(MIÉP) 20
Hungary 12 (fn 11), 16, 20, 31, 34,
43–50, 58, 70–1, 81, 88, 135, 146

identity 5, 7, 65, 130; identity
formation 54; identity politics 34
ideology 4–5, 9, 11, 35, 44–7, 57–9,
61, 63–5, 68–9, 72, 99–100, 125–6,
138; 'end of ideology' 72; host
ideology 61, 68; party ideology
45–6, 49; populist radical right
ideology 6–7, 10–12 (fn 12)
Iglesias, Pablo 65–6, 73
immigrants 8, 21, 79, 118, 122, 131–2,
135, 146–7, 150; anti-immigrant
sentiments 13, 119; illegal
immigrants 8, 46
immigration 10–16, 21, 54, 57, 68,
71–3, 120, 131, 139, 146, 150, 150;
anti-immigration 48, 150;
integration 14, 119, 131
Independent Greeks (ANEL) 95, 100,
107
Indignados 66
Information 144 (fn 1)
International Monetary Fund (IMF)
111, 113
Internet 73, 122, 143
Iran 101
Ireland 7–8, 12 (fn 11), 20, 44, 70, 82,
88; constitution 6
Irish Republican Army (IRA) 132
Isayev, Andrei 24
Islam 119–21, 137–9; Quran 137
Islamic Salvation Front (FIS) 133
Islamophobia 84, 119, 122, 137, 140,
143–7; anti-Islam sentiments 118,
120; anti-Muslim 118

Israel 26, 135, 138
issues 10, 13–16, 34–5, 45–6, 57–8,
68, 72, 119–20, 131, 138;
(position) ownership 10–12 (fn 14),
34–5; saliency 10–11, 45; socio-
cultural 10, 16, 34, 72; socio-
economic 10, 34, 72
Italian Social Movement (MSI) 33
Italy 9, 12 (fn 11), 16, 21, 23, 31, 34,
39, 58, 70–1, 78, 88–90, 108, 111
Italy of Values-List di Pietro 90

Jalkh, Jean-Fran ois 40
Jensen, Siv 121
#JeSuisCharlie 141–2
Jewish Defence League (JDL/LDJ)
130, 135, 138
Jews 47, 138–40; Jewish community
141; Jewish Museum (Brussels)
137
Jones, Owen 112
Juncker, Jean-Claude 53, 55, 79, 81–2,
93

Kaczyński brother (Lech and
Jarosław) 16, 48, 58, 111, 147
Kahane, Meir 130
Kappel, Barbara 40
Keita, Ibrahim Boubacar 142
King Abdullah II 142
Kjærsgaard, Pia 117
Klingemann, Hans-Dieter 3, 9
Kopecký, Petr 103
Korwin-Mikke, Janusz 39, 41, 42
(fn 1), 94; Coalition for Renewal of
the Republic – Liberty and Hope
(KORWiN) 42 (fn 1)
Kosovo 84
Kovács, Béla (KGB la) 24
Krugman, Paul 21, 50 (fn 4), 100

Laclau, Ernesto 57
Labour Party (Malta, PL/MLP) 87
Latvia 12 (fn 11), 20–2 (fn 2), 44, 53,
84, 88, 90
Lavrov, Sergei 23

National Popular Front (ELAM) 108
National Socialist Underground 49,
134
nativism 6, 8, 11, 22, 37 (fn 4), 48, 56
Nazism (Nazis) 5, 19, 63, 119, 133–4;
neo-Nazis 37, 81
Netherlands, the 5, 9, 12 (fn 11), 30–1,
34, 44, 65, 70, 77, 80, 82, 88–91,
105, 117–20, 126, 130, 144-5, 150;
Balkenende IV 54
New Democracy (ND) 104, 109
New Flemish Alliance (N-VA) 95
New Majority (NOVA) 95
New Statesman 100
Newsweek 30
New York Times 21, 50 (fn 4), 67, 143
Non-Inscrits (NI) 35–6,
normal pathology (thesis) 3–6, 9–12,
17, 54
Northern Ireland 132
Northern League (LN) 23, 25–6, 31,
36, 39–40, 94–5, 108
Norway 70–1, 121–7, 149; Oslo 121,
125; Ut ya 121, 125
NRC Handelsblad 144 (fn 1)

Obama, President 150
Obermayr, Franz 40
Occupy Wall Street 66
Open Democracy 144 (fn 1)
Orbán, Viktor 16, 20–1, 28, 41, 43–50
(fn 7), 58, 63, 71, 111, 146–7, 150
Order and Justice (TT) 25, 41, 70, 94,
111
Ordinary People and Independent
Personalities (OL'aNO) 95
Orenstein, Mitchell 27
Ortega, Daniel 114

Panhellenic Socialist Movement
(PASOK) 69, 102, 104, 108–9
Papandreou, Andreas 108
Pappas, Takis 108
Paris 26, 137–8, 142–3, 149–51
Paris Saint Germain (PSG) 138
party family 10, 13, 43, 45, 47

Party for Freedom (PVV) 23, 25–6,
36, 39–40, 70, 73, 83, 94, 104–5,
117, 145
Party of Free Citizens (*Svobodn*) 41
Pathological normalcy (thesis) 3,
9–11, 17, 54
PATRIOT ACT 151–2
People-Animals-Nature (PAN) 112
People's Party – Dan Diaconescu (PP-
PD) 70–1
Philippot, Florian 40
pluralism 62, 68, 141
Podemos (We Can) 44, 57, 61–2,
65–6, 70–3, 108
Poland 12 (fn 11), 16, 26, 44, 48, 58,
70–1, 77, 88, 111, 119, 143, 147
Political Capital 25
political dissatisfaction 16, 20–1, 72,
91, 113, 152; *Politikverdrossenheit*
(political apathy) 9
political parties 5, 9, 15, 43–6, 49, 54,
57, 71, 89, 122, 138; flash parties
91
Pope Francis 144
Popular Orthodox Rally (LAOS)
31–2, 89
populism 6–8, 11, 16, 37 (fn 4), 46,
48, 53–4, 57–9, 61–3, 65, 67–9,
71–2, 88, 99; left-wing populism
62–3; right-wing populism 63
populist parties 17, 53–5, 62, 64, 69,
71–3, 107, 114; agrarian populist
parties 69; left-wing populist
parties 57, 108; right-wing populist
parties 64
populist radical right parties 4–5, 8,
10–17, 20–1, 54, 114; impact of 13,
15, 48 (see also radical right
parties)
Populist Zeitgeist 53–4
Portugal 12 (fn 11), 20, 69, 81, 88,
111–13; Assembly of the Republic
112
'Portugal Ahead' 111
Portuguese Communist Party (PCP)
111–12